CHINA'S GREATEST POET

IN THE FOOTSTEPS OF DU FU

CHINA'S GREATEST POET

IN THE FOOTSTEPS OF DU FU

MICHAEL WOOD

SIMON & SCHUSTER

London · New York · Sydney · Toronto · New Delhi

MMXXIII

Frontispiece image: Du Fu for our times – a CG model by Hu Zihan.

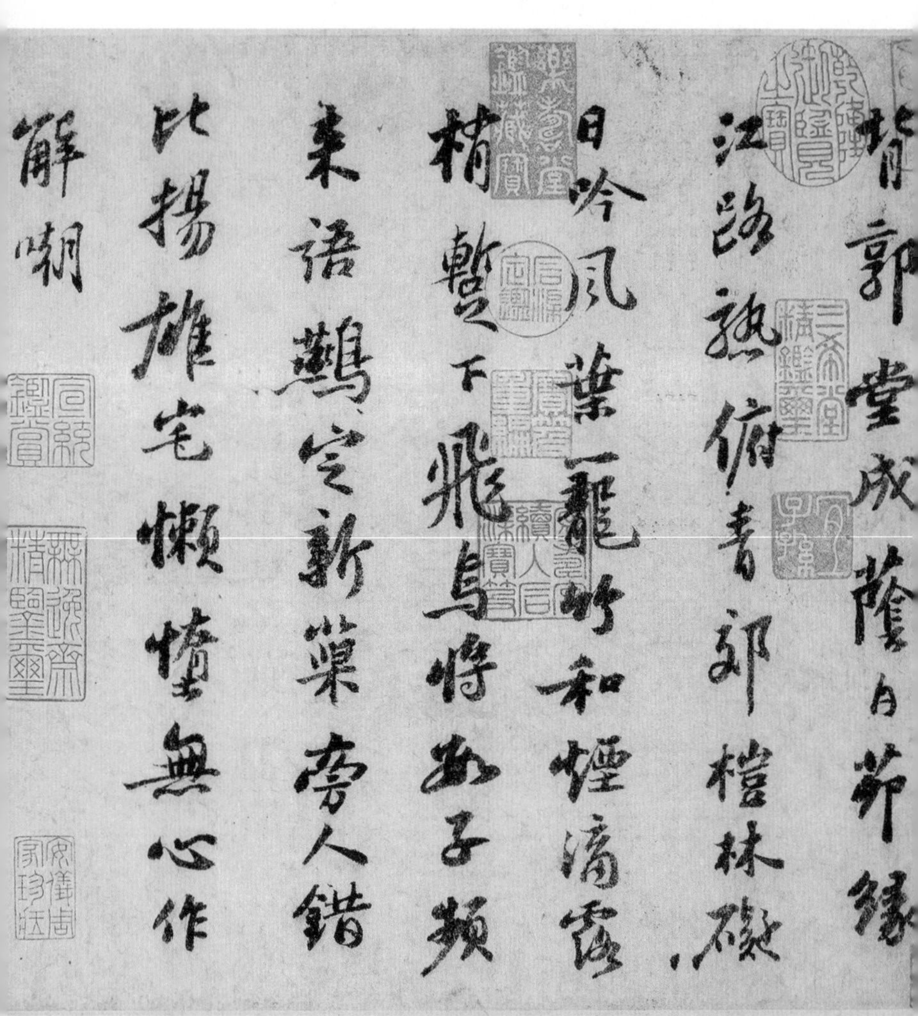

Du Fu's Chengdu poem 'My Cottage is Finished' in the calligraphy of the Song Dynasty poet Su Shi.

Contents

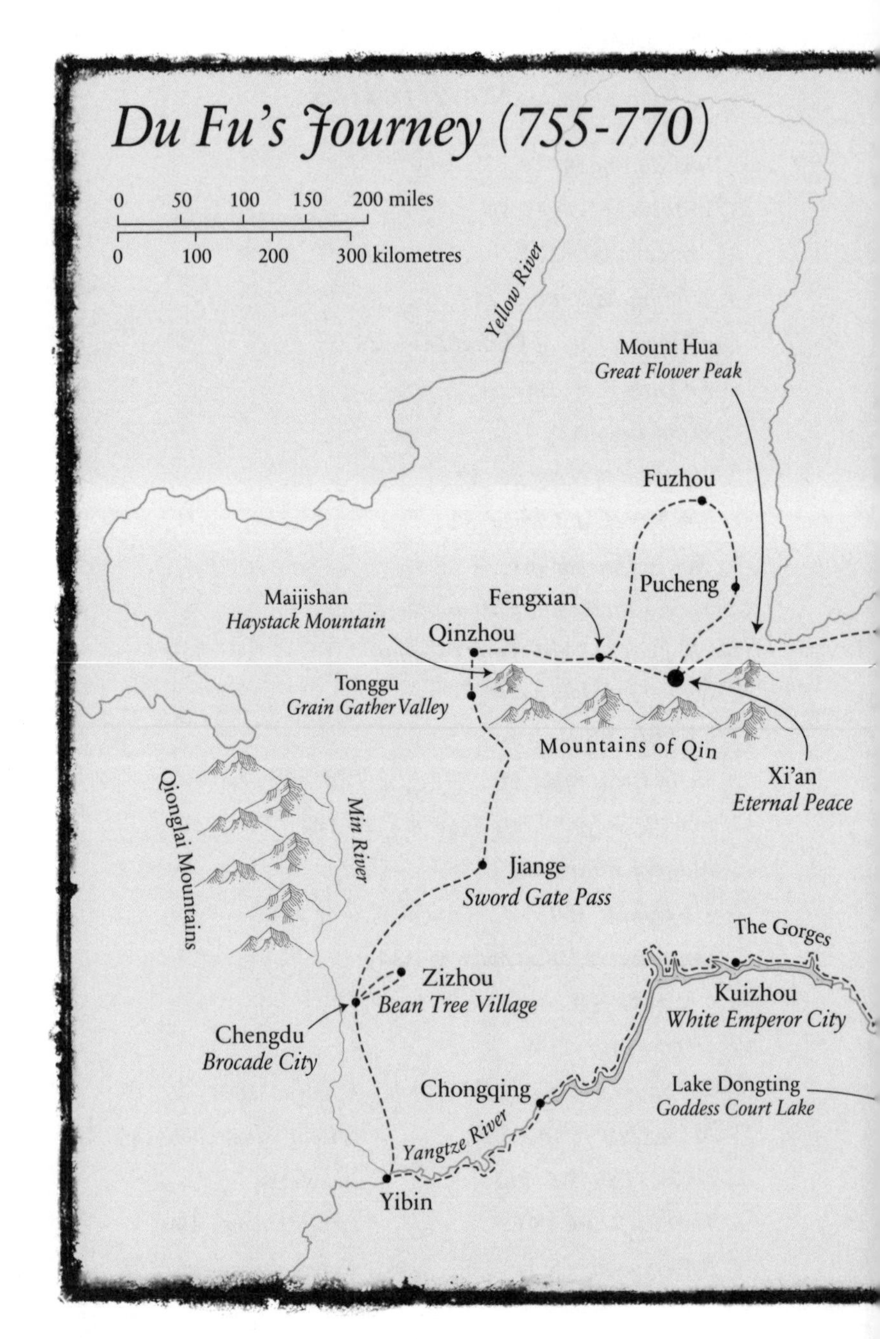
Du Fu's Journey (755-770)
0 50 100 150 200 miles
0 100 200 300 kilometres
Yellow River
Mount Hua
Great Flower Peak
Fuzhou
Pucheng
Fengxian
Maijishan
Haystack Mountain
Qinzhou
Tonggu
Grain Gather Valley
Mountains of Qin
Xi'an
Eternal Peace
Qionglai Mountains
Min River
Jiange
Sword Gate Pass
The Gorges
Zizhou
Bean Tree Village
Kuizhou
White Emperor City
Chengdu
Brocade City
Chongqing
Lake Dongting
Goddess Court Lake
Yangtze River
Yibin

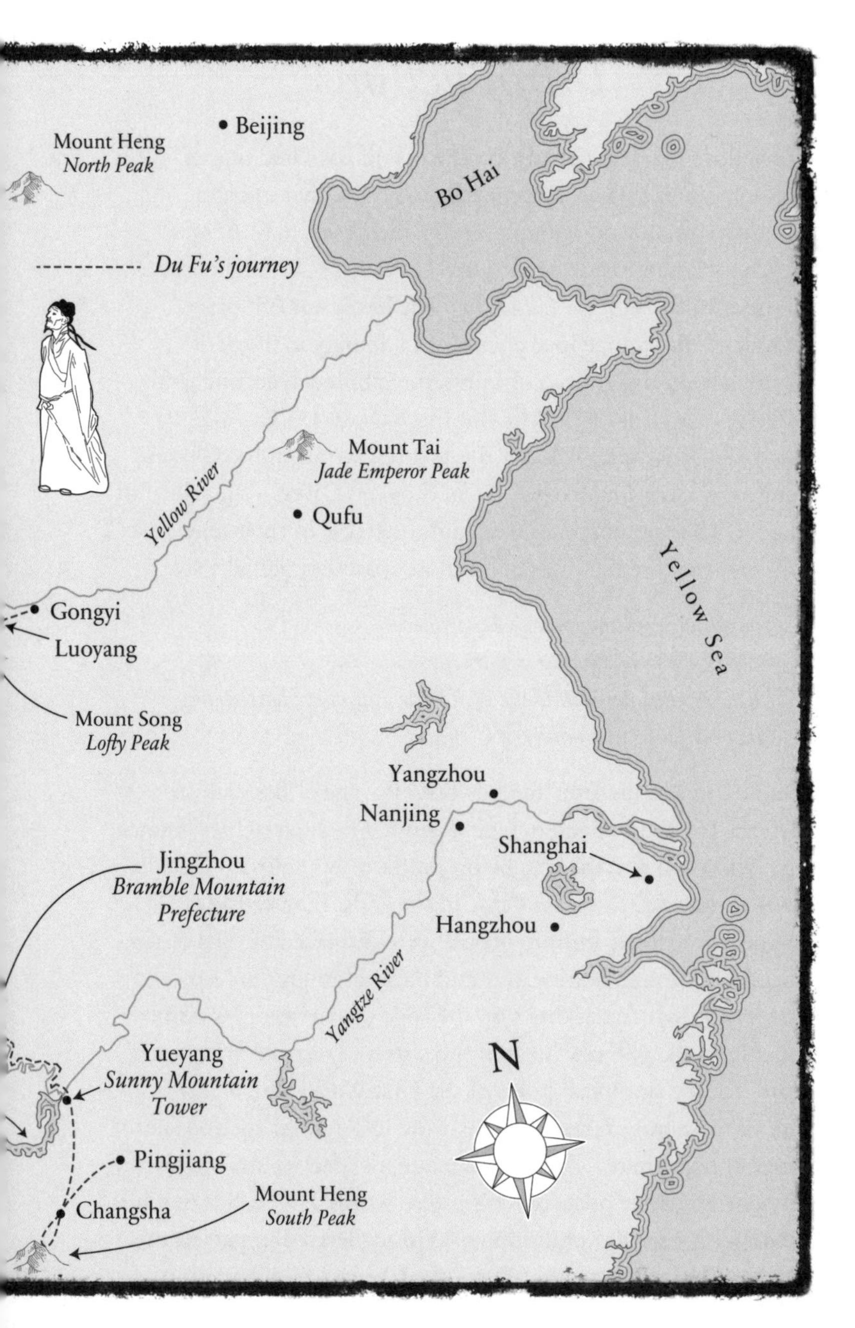
Beijing
Mount Heng
North Peak
Bo Hai
Du Fu's journey
Mount Tai
Jade Emperor Peak
Yellow River
Qufu
Yellow Sea
Gongyi
Luoyang
Mount Song
Lofty Peak
Yangzhou
Nanjing
Shanghai
Jingzhou
Bramble Mountain
Prefecture
Hangzhou
Yangtze River
N
Yueyang
Sunny Mountain
Tower
Pingjiang
Changsha
Mount Heng
South Peak

Introduction

If you love literature of any kind, you will have had one of those moments when you encounter a book that opens a window onto a world you never dreamed existed. Mine was at school when I first encountered Du Fu in A. C. Graham's wonderful *Poems of the Late T'ang*. The book was full of wonders: the strange love poems of Li Shangyin, the dark Baudelairean imaginings of Li He, the fabulously laconic and allusive quatrains of Du Mu. But the star was Du Fu (712-70), with whose *Autumn Wastes* – the 'greatest words in the Chinese language' according to the scholar Stephen Owen – the selection begins. The opening lines were unforgettable in their tangled imagery that seem to hint at far more than they actually say.

The autumn wastes are each day wilder:
Cold in the river the blue sky stirs.
I have moored my boat to the Well Rope Star of the barbarians,
Sited my house in a village of Ch'u . . .

Du Fu lived in the later Tang dynasty, the age of Beowulf in Britain. It was an epoch in China defined by huge achievements in civilization and the arts, before warfare and natural disasters caused massive societal collapse in the 750s. Tang censuses suggest over thirty million people were displaced or died during this time through famine, war and internal migration. Among the refugees, living at times on the edge of starvation, was the poet himself, who saw horrors and survived terrible privations. And like the European poets of the First World War, it was out of these huge contradictions – the lost golden age and the present nightmare – that Du Fu made his greatest art. But also, in contrast to the poets of the western world, Du Fu suffused his work with a secular philosophical vision, derived in part from the meditative practices of Zen – the Chinese transmutation of Indian Buddhism. This nature-mysticism turned even his occasional verses about the minutiae of everyday life into fragments of a vision of extraordinary artistic grandeur, an all-embracing humanism; one man's observation of his world over a lifetime recorded with supreme intelligence and unsparing self-awareness.

Eventually, his health broken, far from home, 'blown like a seagull on the wind', Du Fu died in obscurity; but over the next two or three centuries he became recognised as China's greatest poet, his works collected by the scholars in editions with elaborate textual commentaries. His strong sense of right, and his loyalty to the ideal of a just state, made him the voice of the Confucian ruling elites. His empathy with the common folk turned him into the voice of the Chinese people. Though born into the well-off upper class, he experienced the sufferings of the ordinary man and woman; he spoke for them, and they never forgot it. Since the twelfth century he has been seen as the nation's conscience.

Despite his acknowledged greatness in China, however, Du Fu is still little known in the west. Only a handful of his poems were translated into European languages before the twentieth century, beginning with John Davis, a clerk for the East India Company who as a teenager in Canton became fascinated by Chinese poetry, and in 1829 published a short collection including Du Fu's 'Welcome Rain, Spring Night'. Then, in 1862, twenty poems by Du Fu were translated into French in the pioneering anthology of Hervey de Saint-Denys. Others were very loosely interpreted by the Oriental scholar and poet Judith Gautier in 1867, and Hans Bethge's German versions of some of these (the poems by Li Bai) were the inspiration for the songs in Mahler's song cycle *Das Lied von der Erde* in 1908 – and for many other European composers. The impact of Chinese verse on European modernism, however, really began during the

First World War. This started with the collection of Tang poems in Ezra Pound's *Cathay*, published in April 1915. But Pound's versions were of Li Bai; nor did the great English translator Arthur Waley attempt Du Fu, though he wrote books on Li Bai and Bai Juyi. Florence Ayscough's extraordinary *Autobiography of a Chinese Poet*, published in 1929 with her 'unorthodox', sternly literal, versions of many poems, was the real introduction to the poet in the English-speaking world. The first full translation of Du Fu in any European language was published in German between 1935 and 1939 by the Austrian diplomat and sinologist Erwin von Zach, who was tragically killed in the Second World War. Successful popular translations of Du Fu came only in the second half of the twentieth century, and the first complete translation into English appeared only in 2016. The first volumes of a richly annotated French version by Nicolas Chapuis have now appeared; when complete they will be a treasure trove of western scholarship on Du Fu.

It has taken time, then, but through these translations Du Fu is beginning to be seen as one of the supreme poets of the world. As the poet's American translator Stephen Owen puts it: 'There's Shakespeare, there's Dante, and there's Du Fu: these are poets who created the very values by which poetry is judged; they defined the emotional vocabulary of their culture.' Kenneth Rexroth was even higher in his estimation: 'In my opinion, and in the opinion of a majority of those qualified to speak, Du Fu is the greatest non-epic, non-dramatic poet who has survived in any language. For me his response to the human situation is the only kind of religion likely to outlast this century.' What a ninth-century Chinese critic said then is still true: 'since the dawn of poetry there was no one like him'.

Unlike any great western poet – we might think of Dante's long exiles in Rome and Ravenna or Shakespeare's career mainly in London and Stratford – Du Fu's life in the prime of his creativity was spent as a refugee on the road, moving from place to place. 'My children grew up on the move,' Du Fu wrote, 'and I've left a homestead wherever I have stayed'. Plotted on the map, the epic journey of his later life in a time of war makes a huge arc round the heartland of China. As his fame grew during the Song dynasty (960-1279), his supposed track was marked by memorials in the key places, witnesses to his Chinese odyssey from which he never made it back home to his own personal Ithaca, the family estate with its garden in the hills near Luoyang.

I had been to a few of the sites in his life over the years, paying my respects in the unprepossessing backlot of a secondary school at Yanshi near Luoyang, where a gravestone in what was the family cemetery bears the inscription: 'Du of the Public Works Department', the highest civilian job he held. But, finally, in the rainy autumn of 2019, just as the Covid pandemic was about to break out in China, I set out on the road, following in the footsteps of China's greatest poet. My hope, I suppose, was to see if links still exist between Du Fu's past and our present, and, however imperfectly, to attempt to convey something of his story and his poetry to western readers.

My journey took me from the heartland of the Yellow River Plain to Xi'an, out into Gansu, down into Sichuan to Chengdu and the Yangtze Gorges (the scene of Du Fu's greatest outpouring of poetry), downriver through Hunan to Changsha and the final point in the tiny village of Anding near Pingjiang. It turned out to be a fascinating way to discover the story of a great poet, but also in places to touch an older China, a world both seen and unseen. In our time the past is receding from us at an ever-faster rate, and that is especially so in China, where modernity seems to be triumphing everywhere, even in the deep countryside. But the traveller searching for the meaning of China's ancient culture can still find it in China's present.

For running under the surface are deep currents still shared by Chinese people, and among them is their poetry – the great stream that has sustained the Chinese across the ages, and to which they still give such loyalty. China's is the oldest living poetic tradition on the planet; indeed, the earliest poems in *The Book of Songs,* a wonderful anthology about love, work and war, are older than the *Iliad* and the *Odyssey*. Du Fu's words are at the peak of that tradition, still by common consent expressing part of what it means to be Chinese.

My journey came at a time when the growing impact of catastrophic climate change threatens to destabilise all life on earth. In China in 2020, devastating heatwaves and droughts terrifyingly reduced the river Yangtze to a trickle. It seems to me that these existential threats make the reflections of a man of

the eighth century even more relevant today. Du Fu's themes of friendship and family, of human suffering, of the sustaining and consoling power of nature, of the secular vision of Tang poetry and the cosmic humanism of Zen, speak to a wider world. As his French translator Nicolas Chapuis puts it, his is 'a voice that lives today with a clarity and power that cannot but astonish'. Which is why to trace his track today, and to see what it might reveal, began to take on an increasingly sharp relevance. As I journeyed, it became clear that we really do live in one world, that culture is global, and that great literature breaks across the boundaries of translation to speak to us all.

The landscape of Sichuan crossed by Du Fu and his family in the winter of 765.

1

Birthplace: Gongyi

'My old homeland forever in my thoughts'

Travel in today's China is a whole new experience compared to the drab Russian-style hotels of thirty or forty years ago, with their foreign currency shops and tight restrictions on visitors. These days you can journey across China staying at boutique hotels, backpackers' hostels and even family-run B&Bs with Italian coffee machines and WiFi. My start, though, was not especially auspicious. My quixotic adventure to trace Du Fu's steps began in the rain at his family home near the old 'eastern capital', Luoyang.

That first day I had misgivings that my romantic enterprise was misguided; that his track might have been obliterated. Seeking the past anywhere in China these days can be a trial for the imagination, where the 'new old' is being built all around us, where the older messy reality of Chinese urban life is being wiped away by Party officials and rapacious developers (often the same people).

I stayed in Gongyi, a typical provincial city: blocks of flats, light industry, desultory ring roads full of car repair shops, truckstops and roadhouses serving basic Henan food – quick snacks for people on the move, like *shaobing*, flatbreads stuffed with mung beans, eggs and tofu. Having dumped my bags, I consoled myself that whatever the ongoing destructions of modernity, 'the landscape remains', as Du Fu himself put it. For out there was a first glimpse of the setting of his old home. From my top-floor room at the Huayu Business Hotel, I could see over the townscape and the Luo River to a rain-sodden reef of green hills stretching out to the Yellow River at its confluence with the Luo. The scene was overlooked by a steep hill topped by a fairy-tale pagoda, which now and then teasingly appeared and then disappeared in flurries of rain and cloud; holding out a promise that somehow, like a river under the ice, running below the surface, the past might, as if by magic, still rise.

Next morning, hunched against rain and wind, I walked along a long flood embankment looking over the thickets by the Luo, where waving willows were shaken and tossed by the storm. On the banks fishermen crouched patiently under umbrellas, their fishing lines, fine as single-haired brushstrokes, disappearing in the turbid flow. At the confluence, the Yellow River turns into a vast ochre flood, opening out as wide as the horizon. This is an axial place in the Chinese story. Close by to the south is Mount Song, the sacred mountain from time immemorial; the middle point of the Middle Land, the *zhongyuan*, the heartland of Chinese civilization which gives their country its name: *zhongguo*. So, a great place to think of the glories of the Chinese past, but also its tragedies: the terrible power of the Yellow River floods that on dozens of occasions have swept away whole provinces and entire cities. A place to contemplate the longevity, and the awesome creativity, of Chinese civilization, and yet also the impermanence of human achievement.

The Du clan was said to be from Xiangyang in Hubei, but under the Tang they made their home at Tulou near Shouyang mountain, close to Luoyang, though they also had an estate by the capital. They had some standing: an ancestor was a famous general of the third century; Du's mother was the great-great-granddaughter of the emperor who founded the Tang; his father was a local administrator from a distinguished line, and his paternal grandfather, Du Shenyan, was a poet of some renown in the early years of the Tang dynasty (hence Du's comment that 'poetry ran in our family's blood'). According to tradition, after the death of his mother when he was still an infant, he was

Pen Rest Peak: site of the Du family home near Gongyi.

raised close to Gongyi, where a brick-lined cave survives, cut into a crumbling brown cliff crowned by a tangle of trees. Fittingly for a writer, it's known as 'Pen Rest Peak'.

It was a bleak day when I visited Gongyi, heavy with cloud and persistent drizzle. There were no tourists, no school parties. As the rain pattered on plantains and pomegranate trees, the gardener swept up the wrack of last night's storm with a besom broom. Old photos from the days of the Republic show an impoverished hamlet comprising a sprawl of low brick and thatch buildings reached by a dirt track. A poor family still lived in the cave dwelling until it was turned into a national monument in 1962. In those days, in the brave new world of Mao Zedong, at least until the Cultural Revolution, Du Fu could still be considered a national treasure because of his sympathy for the people – and, of course, his Confucian loyalty to the state. After that the derelict farm buildings were removed and the cave exposed. In front of it now is a big tourist complex, typical of the 'new old' you see everywhere in China these days:

display halls with distressed red vermilion wooden columns, curving roof finials dripping with rain. Inside, life-size dioramas commemorate the shiny-eyed child aged seven, the precocious nine-year-old and the fourteen-year-old genius surrounded by admiring grown-ups – a story of childhood he tells in his somewhat regretful and ironical autobiographical poem, 'Travels in My Prime', translated here in prose by William Hung:

> When I was still only in my seventh year my mind was already full of heroic deeds. My first poem was about the Phoenix, the harbinger of a sagacious reign ... a new age of wisdom. When I was in my ninth year, I began to practise calligraphy in big characters. I'd already written enough poems to fill a satchel. When I was still in my fourteenth year I ventured into the arena of letters and literary masters thought that I resembled Ban Gu and Yang Xiong.

There's a first clue. His first poem. Du Fu carefully crafted his own narrative and as he told it later, his earliest verses (which don't survive) imagined the Phoenix, 'the harbinger of a sagacious reign', imagined in art with its long peacock tails curving and swishing in the light, red-gold and kingfisher blue. Some said the magical bird symbolized the five great qualities taught by Confucius: high virtue, benevolence, honesty, wisdom and civility. It was a creature that only appeared in places and times blessed with utmost peace and happiness, and – in his dreams – the impressionable young Du had seen it. It's a theme he would return to time and again.

Let's imagine the seven-year-old already thrilled by the idea of the imperial presence. Maybe he had even seen the emperor at the peak of his youthful glamour, wearing his dragon robes and being carried on the phoenix sedan chair in procession through the eastern capital of Luoyang. Certainly, we know that Du Fu had already experienced dazzling flashes of the court's high culture. As we shall see, fifty years on, he tells the story of how he had been taken as a child to the house of an imperial kinsman to see a concert of the great court dancer Lady Gongsun. A little later, when he was eleven or twelve, 'more than once' he heard the famous musician Li Guinian, with his 'voice like a demon' playing his seven-stringed *qin* in princely mansions around the capital. From early on he had glimpsed the gilded palanquins and heard the bronze bells and the sonorous musical stones summoning the spirits. However distantly, he had felt the elation of the imperial presence and the aura of majesty, and he carried these indelible memories from Prince Qi's mansion and Lord Cui Jiu's hall back to the house at Gongyi.

Today, among the thickets of bamboo, peaches and pomegranates, the only truly 'old' thing at Du Fu's supposed birth site is the cave: brick-lined, with a small white statue and a vase of plastic flowers. The tour guides say that he was born inside the cave, but it was perhaps only used for storage. His aunt's house itself is long gone; presumably it stood on the flat land between the cliff and the little rivulet below. The museum display gives the orthodox view of Du Fu, developed in the Song dynasty and today pushed by the Communist Party in schools, that he was a true Confucian, 'always thinking of the state', that he loved his family, and had a deep sympathy with the poor during the disasters that swept China in his adult life. To an extent this is true: 'I always followed the Confucian path', he himself said later, though as we shall see there is another far more capacious story – one that reveals his critiques of empire, bad rulers and corruption, as well as his uncanny way of putting himself in the shoes of those who had lost everything.

Amid rumbling thunder and more rain, I took shelter in one of the exhibition halls. A big, dramatically lit diorama serves to remind us of the realism of his war poetry and the power of his political verse. In 'The Ballad of the Army Wagon' the poet

Gongyi, the traditional site of Du Fu's birth.

meets a column of poor conscripts heading off on the road, most never to return. Dust swirls round the river bridge and then comes the famous Kipling-esque exchange, the young squaddie speaking to an upper-class person with the deference of the ordinary soldier the world over:

> This is the way things are. From fifteen you can be sent to guard the north, and at forty you can still be working on the army farms out west... And still the war-loving emperor's dreams of conquest are not finished. But it's kind of you to ask, good sir, I shouldn't express such resentment... Have you heard, out in the west on the shores of Kononor, the bones of the dead lie unburied in drifts under a sky howling with ghosts...

But let's not anticipate the story.

2

Story of a Life

'Poetry was my family's business'

The year he was born here, 712, was the moment of lift-off for China's new golden age. In the first half of his reign, the new emperor Xuanzong oversaw an era of cultural rebirth. He himself was a painter, musician, poet and a patron of libraries and orchestras; so cultured, energetic and sagacious was he that the imperial family later bestowed upon him the title 'The Brilliant Emperor'. It was an exhilarating time: 'Bliss it was in that dawn to be alive,' as Wordsworth would say a thousand years later, and in very different circumstances, 'but to be young was very heaven!' As one whose childhood fed on dreams of peace and order, Du Fu felt much the same: 'Those days,' he recalled later, 'rice was succulent... the granaries were full, and there was not a robber on the road in all the nine provinces of China'.

Of his childhood he tells us very little. His father, a provincial administrator, lived away. As his mother had died (perhaps in childbirth), he never knew her and he was brought up by his aunt, whom he adored. With her we get our first story about him, which comes from a funerary inscription he later wrote for his aunt's grave. When he was a baby there was an outbreak of plague in Henan. A local shamaness visited the house and cast a geomantic spell while Du Fu and his baby cousin lay asleep in the same room. The spirit medium told Du Fu's aunt that only one of these children would survive. Which one? The one lying in the corner of the room where her baby was sleeping. Then (so he says) the aunt moved her own child and put Du Fu in the corner. 'So, my aunt's child died, and I was spared'. An eerie tale. Did it give him a sense that he had been singled out? Predestined for greatness?

Very little verse survives from Du Fu's youth. Of more than 1,400 surviving poems, less than a tenth were written before he was in his forties, and we have none from his first twenty years. Most of the poems we have were composed after the devastating An Lushan rebellion of 755 convulsed the country in an eight-year war in which millions died. It was then that he found his true voice. The war was the turning point of his life and everything he wrote afterwards needs to be seen in that light. For what it is worth, though, in his retrospective self-portrait, the impression he gives us of his youth paints a picture of a privileged self-centred boy from one of the well-off gentry clans, many of whom were subsequently wiped out in the wars of the eighth and ninth centuries. Of his first public readings aged fourteen, he said:

I was temperamental, and I was already over fond of wine.
I needed it to soften an uncompromising hatred of wickedness and hypocrisy. I associated only with wise old greyheads. Exhilarated by wine we cast our glances over the entire universe, and all vulgar worldliness dwindled into oblivion . . .

As a Portrait of the Artist as a Young Man, that rings true to me. He was full of himself, arrogant even, and saw his future path laid out before him. But he was also someone who, from an early age, saw the world as it ought to be, not as it is. Even in good times that can be a recipe for anguish and, worse, heartbreak.

Affectionate reminiscences of his youth, though, are scattered through his later verse:

I remember when I was fifteen, still a child at heart,
Healthy as a brown calf racing all around,
Eighth month in the garden, pears and jujubes ripe;
In one day I shinned up the trees a thousand times . . .

Like many Chinese literati, he had an incredible breadth of reading from an early age. He later wrote many poems on his poetics and on the source of his artistic inspiration. One major source was the *Wen Xuan*, the famous sixth-century anthology of belles-lettres. He had clearly memorized huge chunks of it and quoted from it many times, later urging his own son Zongwu to 'master thoroughly the principles of the *Wen Xuan*'. Apart from that, he frequently mentions major poets of the Six Dynasties period (between the fall of the Han in the third century and the rise of the Sui and the Tang after 589), including poets such as Tao Yuanming, Bao Zhao and Xie Lingyun.

One extraordinarily vivid reminiscence of his youth is an important clue to his childhood sensibility, or so it seems to me at least. Fifty years later Du Fu was invited by the local governor to a concert at the old prefectural town of Kuizhou (today Baidi), at the entrance to the Yangtze Gorges, where he was then living. There he saw a dancer, Madam Li, perform the sword dance: an Iranian or Turkic dance imported along the Silk Road like many other fashions, foods and arts during the expansive days of the High Tang. The circumstances he records with the exact date (15 November 767) in his longest introduction to any of his poems – he often annotated his verses with explanations of how they came to be written – so it appears that this story had unusual significance to him. Deeply moved by her performance, he asked who had taught her, and she replied: Lady Gongsun, the most famous dancer in the golden decade of the Brilliant Emperor. Gongsun had been the greatest artist of the 'Peach Garden': the royal school of dance. By an amazing chance, fifty years before, as a young child not yet five, Du Fu had actually seen Gongsun herself perform, and he gives us a child's-eye description of the dancer, taking us right into the mind and feelings of his young self:

> I remember when I was still a little boy, I saw Gongsun perform the sword dance at Yancheng. For purity of technique and self-

confident attack she was unrivalled in her day. From the 'royal command performers' and the 'insiders' of the Spring Garden and Pear Garden schools in the palace, down to the official 'call dancers' outside, there was no one during the early days of His Sagely Pacific Majesty who understood this dance as she did:

In time past there was a lovely woman called Gongsun
Her sword dance astonished the whole world.
Audiences crowded round awestruck as she danced
And to their reeling senses the world seemed to go on rising and falling long after she had finished dancing
When she bent back you saw nine suns falling, shot down by Yi the god of archers! ...
When she leapt you imagined gods astride flying dragons in the clouds ...
When she advanced you expected thunder and lightning from a gathering storm ...
And when she stopped, you saw the cold light over a vast calm sea ...

He is reproducing here the memory of precisely how *he felt*. For Du Fu, Gongsun presented an unforgettable image of creative freedom and passion, in which the dance became a symbol for all art, whether calligraphy, painting or poetry. Indeed, in his prose introduction to the poem, he tells us in so many words that he saw it as a metaphor; for he mentions that a famous calligrapher, Zhang Xu, had also seen Gongsun dance, 'and after seeing her he used his brush differently, his grass writing calligraphy took flight.' (Grass writing with its spidery tracery is one of the freest of all forms of calligraphy.) For Du Fu, then, Lady Gongsun epitomized artistic expression, with her heady, almost supernatural, combination of control, rhythm and freedom. Remembering the effect this concert had on his five-year-old self, Du Fu perhaps believed he had identified a wellspring of his own poetic sensibility, his creative imagination, and he saw, in whatever medium you worked, the need in the end to cut loose from convention.

3

Youthful Adventures

'I'll never forget my lone boat eastern travels'

In his late teens he went travelling down to the Yangtze delta, to Jiangnan and the sea. (All his life, he later tells us ruefully, he dreamed of sailing across the Yellow Sea to Japan: he never did it, but even at the very end, his poems imagine the world beyond the fairy-tale 'Isles of the Blessed'.) He took a passenger boat down to Jiangsu and Zhejiang, the rich and populous coastal plain of the Yangtze delta. It must have been an eye-opening experience. China in the High Tang was changing; a huge population shift to the south was taking place which saw the rapid growth of the cities of the delta 'where the produce of many nations flowed'. Yangzhou, for example, at the junction of the Grand Canal and the Yangtze, was the home of half a million people in the eighth century, and was proverbially a city of wealth and pleasure, the first place in the world to be lit by artificial lighting at night – a city that never slept. In the delta the harbours were crammed with merchant vessels, and it was

The riches of the South: junks and sampans at Fuzhou, 1902.

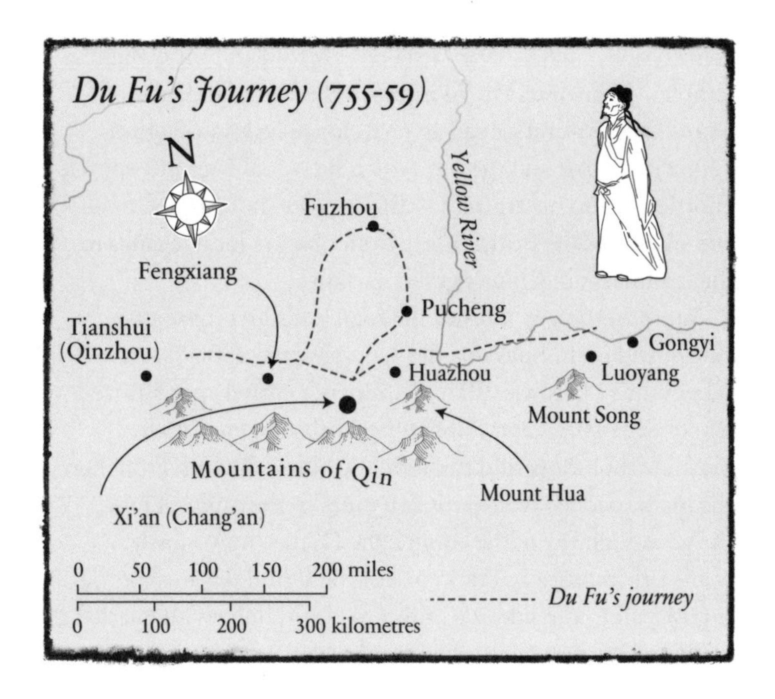

said ten thousand ships were on the move at any one time, 'a circulation that couldn't stop even for a minute'. Here, as in the capital, one had the exhilarating sense of belonging to a great international civilization.

This was a formative journey in his life. Seeing China and its cultures and landscapes for Du Fu was as important to his imaginative world as his astoundingly wide reading. In these days of his youthful wanderings – like a young European aristocrat on the eighteenth-century Grand Tour – he saw the sites of history and myth, from the tombs of the Yellow Emperor and King Yu the Great, to legendary sites of heroes and dragons. He immersed himself in China's ancient traditions, gathering stories. Like any tourist today he admired the famous historical monuments. 'The great Buddhas of Longmen', he wrote later, looking back, 'in their giant gorge cutting through the countryside ... where every vista reveals gold and silver Buddha temples.' The young Du Fu imbibed the myths and tales of China's history and gained an encyclopaedic knowledge of China itself, past and present, which he would later incorporate effortlessly into his art (just as Shakespeare did with the myths and history of the British Isles), from obscure local legends to the landmarks in China's grand narrative.

But for us on our journey the road leads first through Yanshi and on to Luoyang, the Tang 'eastern capital', with its picturesque old town still mercifully not entirely modernized, where wine sellers and calligraphers rub shoulders with machine tool shops and traditional Chinese doctors. From here the main road led westwards 230 miles to the capital. Once the great highway of the empire, the G310 is now mostly a multi-lane motorway, but in places you'll find the ancient route survives off to the side as a minor road still lined with gnarled plane trees with whitewashed trunks. Half-way along is the sacred mountain, Huashan, a great goal for pilgrims then as it still is today.

What the young Du Fu saw here and elsewhere on the roads of Tang China is vividly brought to life in Tang memoirs and travellers' tales. The diary of the Japanese Buddhist pilgrim Ennin, who travelled all round China in the ninth century, gives intimate details of life on the road – the hostels, restaurants, tea houses and waystations. And the people you met in such places are described with Chaucerian exuberance in *The Great Book of Marvels* by Du Fu's contemporary Tai Fu. This was another world from the great ritual events of the court; the festivals, outings and royal audiences described in official sources. This was the life of the streets, with Central Asian cloth dealers, Iranian cake sellers and travelling merchants, like the grain dealer Du Fu describes heading down the Yangtze to Yangzhou. In the pilgrims' inns under Mount Hua, you met healers and

The path up Mount Hua.

fortune tellers, gurus of Tantrism and esoteric Buddhism, Daoist mystics, conjurers and conmen. At night in the hostels you listened to songs, fairy tales and ghost stories: lurid travellers' tales of sexual encounters with apparitions from other worlds. The road was, as Ennin described it, recalling Kipling's Grand Trunk Road, a 'great river of life'. Here, around Huashan, the young Du Fu mingled with the hordes of pilgrims on the road. All human life was there; the unseen transcendent was present in the everyday, always seeping over the threshold into the land of here and now, and here and elsewhere Du Fu forgot none of it. On the road, too, he would have met other hopeful career-minded young examination candidates, would-be officials like him, on their way to the capital. Unbeknown to him, thirty years later he would be back in this neck of the woods in a dead-end job at the nadir of his official career, such as it was, But now he journeyed bursting with youthful optimism. 'I'd read everything and thought I was superb!'

4

Chang'an: City of Eternal Peace

'I remember long ago those were the glory days'

In his mid-twenties he arrived at the capital Chang'an, today's Xi'an, to take the examinations that would allow him to become a government official. He wanted nothing more than to serve the emperor in this new age of wisdom. Chang'an, 'Eternal Peace', was then a world city like Baghdad or Constantinople, a giant five-mile rectangle filled with temples, gardens, orchards and vast wooden palaces rearing over the quarters of low-rise houses. At its heart was the imperial Daming Palace, three times the size of the later Forbidden City in Beijing – whose main southern entrance, the enormous brick and wood Danfeng Gate – has been spectacularly reconstructed for today's visitor just north of the surviving Ming walls. The parks and gardens of the palace with their ornamental lakes were artificial landscapes laid out for the delectation of the royal family and the nobles on their summer picnics. The bustling markets to the south were crowded with foreign merchants from Persia, India, Central Asia, Korea and Japan. The wards were full of Buddhist temples crammed with gorgeous statuary and wall paintings by great artists. City life was a round of festivals: Daoist, Buddhist, folk deities and imperial anniversaries. On All Souls Festival, the Japanese pilgrim Ennin says, 'all the monasteries of the city made flower-scented candles, flowery cakes, artificial flowers, fruit trees and the like, vying with each other in their rarities. The custom is to spread them all out as offerings in front of the Buddha halls and the citizens go around all the monasteries and perform the rituals ... The whole city comes to worship.'

For Du Fu, the city would a play special part in his imagination. It was a city of the mind as much as a concrete reality. A vision of order and auspiciousness, laid out as a cosmic map shaped like the Big Dipper, it embodied a dream of civilization, as he recalled longingly in his years in exile. Today all that has gone. For the modern traveller in search of Tang Chang'an there are only a few signs. In places today's Ming walls preserve the layout of the city of the eighth century, but there are scant vestiges in the streets of the life that he saw: an old Daoist temple in the street of funeral shops beyond the East Gate where fortune tellers sit at their little tables with the *I Ching* and yarrow stalks; or the Wolong shrine just inside the city wall off Baishulin Street, in a neighbourhood of junk shops and art stalls. Founded over 1,800 years ago in the Han, this temple was turned into a machine tool shop in the Cultural Revolution, but today what is left has been restored and is again open for worship, its bells ringing over its little neighbourhood.

Wolong temple, Xi'an, once home of a famous painting by Wu Daozi.

In Du Fu's day the shrine was home to a celebrated mural painting of the goddess Guanyin by the Tang artist, Wu Daozi, the 'Sage of Painting.' Wu was an older contemporary of Du Fu; the master of illusion, he was so celebrated that he became the subject of legends, and gifted with supernatural powers. It was even said that in the end he disappeared through a door into his own painting, never to be seen again. In Du Fu's youth 'numerous artists of amazing ability gathered in the capital' to make public art as well as royal and noble commissions. Later ages viewed it as the golden age of Chinese art and Wu was the star, producing works like the huge mural in Great Harmony Hall in Datong Palace in the 740s. Renowned for his impressionistic techniques Wu, it was said, 'never looked back and will have no successors'. None of his paintings survive, but murals in recently excavated Tang royal and noble tombs show his influence, especially on the sarcophagus of Empress Zhenshun from 737 with its startling, almost abstract panels of mountainscapes. 'Bold and free as the sea … Wu brought the art of painting to a pinnacle', as a ninth-century critic Zhang Yanyuan put it, 'in a blaze of splendour with completeness as its goal'.

Du Fu was a passionate admirer. 'There are many famous master painters in the past,' he wrote, 'but the art of Master Wu by far excels them all. He shifts the very axis of the Earth, and makes the scene pulse with exquisite energy on the palace walls.' Wu had first learned his brushwork from the 'wild man' calligrapher, Zhang Xu, whose explosive cursive script as we have seen had been inspired by seeing a performance of the sword dance by that same Lady Gongsun who had so captivated Du Fu. 'Wu demonstrated that the use of the brush in calligraphy and in painting are the same,' Zhang Yanyuan wrote: 'while others fix their attention on coherent outlines, he split and scattered dots and strokes; while others rigidly imitate the likeness of things, he rids himself of such vulgarity. With just one or two strokes, the image comes to life. His dots and lines are disjoined, at times even missing. This shows that while the stroke may be incomplete, the mind (*yi*) is fully captured'.

There were profound lessons in this for the young Du Fu. Poetry, calligraphy and painting were intimately tied together as the 'Three Perfections' (as the Emperor Xuanzong himself called them). The process of reading a picture, filling in the blank spaces, was akin to interpreting a poem. Like many Tang poets, Du Fu was fascinated by these new ideas and techniques, and through his life he wrote many poems about the art of painting; indeed a Song writer described his poems as 'paintings without forms'. In one he looks back to his early days in Chang'an seeing a magical mural landscape: 'a magnificent painting of the immortal peak of Fangu on a white wall in the lofty hall in Chang'an'. The Yangtze Gorges in particular were a special subject for artists, as Du Fu records: 'I recall long ago in Xianyang in the capital market a time when paintings of mountains and rivers were spread for sale. There once the Wu Gorges appeared on a precious screen, as for the Chu palace still I face the sapphire peaks and wonder.'

These lines from a longer poem, 'Viewing a Painting of Min Mountain and the Tuo River', are typical of Du Fu's attention to the detail of painting, his scrutiny of images, changing textures, surface and essence:

The River Tuo hangs over the midst of the guests
Min Mountain has come to the northern hall
White-capped waves blow on plaster walls...
Snow clouds, in flux, adorn the scene, and the plants in the sand
lend a distant blur.
Geese on summits follow the brush tip, on the river a rainbow
drinks light from white silk.
A sifting haze of red, isle blossoms in confusion, a brushing of
eyebrow-black, rock-vines stretch long...
As a work of painting, the achievement is rare....

None of Wu Daozi's paintings survive, but this copy of a copy conveys the swirling energy that so impressed Du Fu and his contemporaries.

Wild Goose Pagoda, Xi'an: scene of Du Fu's vision in 752.

However distant, we might compare poets' responses to the Impressionist painters in late nineteenth-century Europe; Rilke for example said the supreme influence on his poetry was Cezanne's painting. In Du Fu's day the temples and palaces of Chang'an were repositories of the latest art, as well as of the productions of antiquity – and here too it was 'modern art' that most thrilled the artists and literati.

A few yards from the Wolong shrine down a leafy backstreet you come to the city wall. Steps lead up onto the wide wall walk, from where you can see across the modern rooftops towards the elegant towers of the Buddhist shrines south of the Ming walls, the only major surviving fabric of Tang Chang'an. Pride of place is the Wild Goose Pagoda, till not so long ago standing amid open fields with cabbage patches and crumbling brick barns, but now engulfed by the expanding city. A great honey-brown brick tower originally 200 feet high, the pagoda was built to house the sutras brought from India by the renowned Buddhist pilgrim Xuanzang back in the 640s, in the heyday of the great emperor Taizong. Du Fu climbed it in autumn 752 and wrote a famous poem about the incident. As he tells us, looking through the window over the vista of the capital, he felt a kind of existential panic, transfixed by an overwhelming fear that the glory of the Tang civilization could vanish like an insubstantial vision; the solid world suddenly crumbling before his eyes. But that again is to run ahead of ourselves in the story.

The year now is 733. Du Fu has turned twenty and Emperor Xuanzong is at the height of his fame and glory. It was the place to arrive as a young man with the world at your feet, armed with a book satchel, his leather arm rest, brushes, ink stone and ink block. Normally a new arrival would take lodgings in one of the taverns and hostels around the East Market – wisest, perhaps, in view of the gruelling nature of the exams – but maybe he stayed with relatives on the Du family estate south of the city and rode into the exam halls every day.

For today's traveller there are modern chain-hotels, serving hearty breakfasts of Shaanxi and Sichuan food, sweet persimmon cakes, thick scrolls of hot 'Biangbiang' noodles and (a favourite of Du Fu) cold *liang pi*, slippery noodles with slivered cucumbers in chilli oil; enough to set you up for the whole day. Looking over the rooftops from the terrace of my hotel near the south gate, it's a place to reflect on the way the capital loomed so large in Du Fu's imagination. It was somewhere to aspire to, to reach, and to get back to: the city on the hill. 'It is said the city is like a chess board', he wrote, meaning perhaps both physically in its grid shape, and also as a metaphor; a constantly changing game of courtly advancement and retreat, promotion and exclusion. Later its loss became etched in his mind, the path to preferment which for him was once so clear and seemingly certain; to get the ear of the emperor; to be an adviser; to have one's portrait hung in the Unicorn Hall along with the great ministers of the past; to have one's verses read to the emperor himself, copied by a famous calligrapher. To be looked up to by the court literati. In a culture that so revered the written word, and poetry above all, no accolade could be greater.

But when he sat the exams, a three-day marathon in a cubicle with a table, board and latrine bucket, he failed. It was a turning point in his life, a story he tells in two different long poems, lines from which I have combined:

In the prime of life, I was sent by my home prefecture to sit the state examinations…
I feared no rival among the competing scholars…
nor any difficult questions that might be put to me…
Wielding my writing brush like a god.
I thought of course that I was extraordinary
And should immediately climb to the top…
And restore the purity of culture and civilization.
But those hopes ended in bleak despair

His failure was a big blow, undermining his sense of who he was, and who he felt he was destined to be. Why someone so gifted failed has been debated endlessly ever since by scholars in China. The likeliest reason is simply that he was just too sure of himself, too arrogant perhaps, refusing to knuckle down to the strict requirements of the examinations, to give the examiners what they wanted. But one can overanalyse; the fact was that exam competition was very tough and there were many outstanding candidates. Maybe he just didn't cut it? At any rate, this failure in a sense is the moment that begins his wanderings, his life as a 'sojourner'.

He goes travelling again. 'I got to know all the nine provinces of China,' he says. His journeys led him north to one special

Emperor Xuanzong, poet, artist and musician – playful before the fall.

place of pilgrimage: Qufu, the birthplace of Confucius. Others had made the same journey, among them the historian Sima Qian when he was a young man, 'learning the laws of Lu'. Even further back in time Confucius himself had travelled across the warring states of China, 'learning the ways of men'. Born well over 1,000 years before Du Fu's day, Confucius had shaped the core values of Chinese civilization, or as he put it, 'this culture of ours'. For him the social ideal is harmony and stability under a virtuous ruler, and each person has a role to play in helping the emperor achieve this common good. Confucius was a huge influence on Du Fu; 'my way was the Confucian Way', he stated near the end of his life. We have to take that overt acknowledgement at face value, looking back over his wild youth – the hunts, the drinking parties, the nights spent with mystics and renouncers, seeking consolations for the wounded anxious heart. In his last poem he speaks of the primacy for him of 'music and rites', the basis of Confucian teaching; this was his moral and cultural anchor.

5

An Early Poem

'Contemplating Mount Tai'

But, of course, Confucius was not the only influence. The mystical perceptions and practices of Daoism were important to Du Fu from the start. So too was that distinctively Chinese synthesis of Daoism and Buddhism, Chan – what we call Zen. Following a number of Japanese scholars of Zen, the translator David Hinton has suggested that Du Fu studied Zen at this time, maybe at the feet of the famous monk Shenhui (684-*c.*758), the 'Great Teacher' who was the founder of Chinese Zen. Shenhui was living outside Nanyang south of Luoyang in the Longxing monastery, the 'ancestral home of Zen' which still stands today. Some have questioned Hinton's interpretation of the paramount influence of Zen on Tang poetry in general (and in the case of Wang Wei and Du Fu in particular), but the terminology suffuses Du Fu's poetry, and in several poems he specifically talks about Zen ideals, and his failure to live up to them. 'I basically adhere to Kashyapa', he wrote later of the ancestral teacher of Zen, 'but the golden scalpel shaved my eyeballs in vain: I have never freed myself from the images in the mirror'. The scholar of Buddhism R. H. Blyth wrote long ago: 'Zen naturally finds its readiest expression in poetry rather than philosophy because it has more affinity with feeling than with intellect; its poetic predilection is inevitable'. Zen, then, can be a key to poetry – and poetry a key to Zen.

From this time, we can place what is perhaps Du Fu's first surviving poem, written when he was twenty-four in 736 (remember again that his oeuvre is curated: we must assume that it is his decision that we may have nothing before this

Mount Tai, king of mountains.

time). The poem is called 'Contemplating Mount Tai' and presumably came from his travels around China up to Shandong in the mid-730s. It shows that he had already imbibed Daoist and Zen ideas. On the surface it is deceptively simple, as if the poem were just a snapshot of a sacred mountain with a description of its natural scenery. While on one level that is true, the poem is more layered in a way that is notoriously difficult to translate. Here's a literal version of 'Contemplating Mount Tai', following David Hinton's translation:

The king of mountains; how to describe?
Through the whole of Chi and Lu never lose sight of its greenness
In it Creation has concentrated all that is numinous and beautiful
Yin and yang (northern and southern slopes) divide the dawn from the dark

Heaving chest brings forth layered clouds
Homing birds enter bursting eyes
Really must stand on top of the highest peak
And in a single glance take in all the other mountains so small

Had he apparently not climbed it at this point? The poem is ambiguous on that, but that is how it is usually understood: he is contemplating, imagining the view from the top. The fifth and sixth lines are well known for their very unusual word order. David Hawkes's literal reading is:

Heaving breast are born layered clouds
Burst eye-sockets enter returning birds

Hawkes notes that this kind of inversion (in Chinese, *dao zhuang*) is seen by Chinese critics as 'extremely daring and bizarre' (as the Chinese language has no grammatical inflections, the word order is generally crucial in determining meaning through syntactical relationship). It is interesting to see Du Fu this early on trying these poetic devices, as he will later in his career, more and more startlingly, pushing the reader to the limits of interpretation. Such an altered or disrupted word order – 'deranged' is Hawkes's word for it – at times leads to unresolvable ambiguities. Is the 'heaving breast' the mountain as a living presence (akin, one might say, to the 'deep breathing' mountain Wordsworth imagines in *The Prelude*) which gives birth to layers of cloud? As anyone who has climbed Taishan knows, a heaving breast is a condition of the 'lung-busting' steep climb; while 'bursting eyes' recalls the American expression 'eye-popping'. As for 'returning birds', traditionally the pilgrim climbs in the evening to watch dawn from the mountaintop, so in the early part of the climb at dusk, you can see birds flying home below you. At the summit, when you greet the dawn, often layered clouds do indeed lie below the climber, giving the impression that they have been exhaled by the peak itself.

'Layered clouds' from the summit of Mount Tai.

Taishan is one of the Sacred Five holy peaks especially revered by Daoists. (On my travels in the 1980s, I met Daoist recluses, hermits and nuns who had lived wild in lonely valleys on Songshan all the way through the communist revolution.) Hinton suggests Daoist and Zen ideas were already working on the young Du Fu's creative imagination when he wrote this in his mid-twenties. In later life, with a wife and family, driven to and fro by war, he had no time or opportunity to study, so it makes sense that it was in his twenties that he sat at the feet of Zen masters, beginning the path to enlightenment.

6

Wanderings

'In the blue sky my wings failed me'

He later constructs a self-referential narrative of this time, which purports to be true but cannot be the whole story. He says he was only concerned with poetry slams and drinking bouts, young men's games and pastimes. He tells the tale with ironical, self-mythologizing relish. This translation is by William Hung:

The next few years I played and roamed
In the spring I sang on the terraces where the poets competed...
Summer I hunted among the green hills,
in the winter I whistled for the falcons in the Purple Oak forests
... and chased wild beasts on Cloud and Snow Ridge...
I trailed my hems wherever sweet ale was served, and drank myself sick...

The old city of Kaifeng is one of the places where tradition says the poets competed. Today, if you walk beyond the station into a wooded park, close to the giant Fanta pagoda and a lovely shrine to Yu the Great, you'll find a terrace where Li Bai, Du Fu and Gao Shi are supposed to have jousted in their poetry slams, throwing out random rhymes to be picked up, played with and passed round in games of wit, skill and speed of thought.

We don't know how he kept himself during this time. Clearly he had private wealth, an income drawn from the family estates. Was he also cultivating wealthy patrons who valued poetry so highly and could already see his great talent? Or perhaps he leaned on brothers, cousins and uncles in his wide extended family as he did in his later life? Either way, he says later that he became angry with himself for 'hanging on the coat tails of the rich'.

Male sport: 'The next few years I played and roamed'.

Eventually, still hoping to make his name as a poet, he journeyed back to Luoyang. In 740 his father and his aunt died, and Du Fu stayed in the family area for three years to fulfil his filial mourning duties. And it was there in 744 that he met the great poet of the age, Li Bai. A friendship soon blossomed with the older man. Li Bai was a brilliant devil-may-care roisterer who'd fought out in the west, a Daoist libertine where Du Fu in outward life was temperamentally a dutiful Confucian – though both would end up being outsiders. The Chinese today love them as a pair – in the Ming dynasty you could buy cheap printed selections of 'Li-Du' at bookstalls in river ports, as we would paperbacks in train stations. It is as if together they represent two sides of the Chinese character: individualism, mysticism and excess on the one hand; duty, family and rootedness on the other.

Life took on a sudden new intensity for Du Fu. The younger man was caught up in the whirlwind of Li Bai's social life, vying with each other to turn out sparkling verses. Du Fu was closely observing Li Bai's poetic tricks, noting the way he told stories, juxtaposing the personal with the cosmic, his precision of feeling. Anyone can generalize, but as William Blake put it: 'to particularise is the alone distinction of merit.' For a year or so they travelled together: 'walking everywhere hand in hand', visiting mountain caves to sit at the feet of Daoist masters, and even 'sleeping under the same thin quilt, their feet entangled'. As in the medieval west, intense male friendship was a feature of civilized society.

Then Li Bai vanished from his life. We don't know why, although there are hints that this may have been deliberate on Li Bai's part. As far as we know, Du Fu saw him again in 745, but never after that, though he tells us he dreamed about him:

Separation by death, in the end you get over.
Separation in life is a continuing grief.
No word from your old friend but you've been in my dreams
as if you know how much I miss you.
I feel as if you are no longer mortal, the distance between us
is so great
The setting moon spills light on the ceiling, for a moment I think
it's your face.
The waters are deep, the waves are wide...
Don't let the river gods take you.

This time was a real learning curve for Du Fu: seeing the landscape and gathering the stories of China; acquiring the skills of a poet; experiencing deep friendship and loss. Just as

Shakespeare emerged as a poet after a seven-year gap in his life of which we know nothing, Du Fu's thirties are a mystery, compounded by the shape of his surviving works in which there is a heavy bias towards poetry written after the early 750s, when famine and civil war turned his world upside down. By then he had also acquired a profound knowledge of Zen Buddhism – not just a passing interest, but (as we have seen) a deep experiential conversance with the practices, and even the technical vocabulary, something which cannot be casually borrowed. He had become an adept, so it is safe to assume that in this period of life, before his marriage, the birth of his five children and the beginning of his enforced wanderings, he had spent time in monasteries, sitting at the feet of masters. And with that we must remember too that there came an intense refinement of perceptions of the rhythms of nature and the cosmos, and by the time he emerges as a great poet in the 750s this is in the very essence of his sensibility. Communion with the cosmos is a key to much of Tang poetry, but of all the poets it is perhaps strongest in Du Fu.

In 746 Du Fu moved back to the capital to attempt to resurrect his official career. Residing in the city, he sat and failed the imperial exam again; this time, like all the candidates, he was blocked by a corrupt chief minister. So he resolved to send writings – a treatise on literature – directly to the emperor, and to his amazement the emperor read it and was impressed, recommending his officials to look into his case. 'I'm an overnight success!' Du Fu wrote sarcastically.

At last, he had a job at court, but it was as a low-level official: an attendant some way down the ranks of the enormous imperial bureaucracy. But at least his meagre stipend enabled him to marry and start a family. In around 752, by now aged forty – late for a Chinese person of that time – he married. His wife, Madame Yang, who must have been quite a few years younger than him, was the daughter of a minister and descendant of an emperor. They would go on to have three sons and two daughters, of whom more soon. But his fledgling career was about to be swept away by events beyond his control.

In the early 750s he emerged as an accomplished poet, recognized by his peers. His poems of this period also begin to exhibit a strong social conscience. From around 750 one of his earliest surviving verses forms part of a group of 'frontier poems': a set of nine poems dealing with the lot of soldiers conscripted to fight in the frontier battles of the early 750s – a theme already powerfully tackled by Li Bai. It's written from the soldier's perspective, criticizing the expansionist policies of the time along with the brutality of conscription, poor peasants 'snared by the law'. It takes the form of a kind of ballad popular since the Han dynasty:

With heavy hearts we quit our village home,
To go to far, far, Turfan River.
There is a set term for service,
Deserters will be punished with death.
The emperor's land is already vast,
What use is therein extending its boundaries?
Parted forever from our parents' love,
Swallowing our sobs, we shoulder arms and march on.

But his job was a dead end, and he soon became disillusioned. 'I have no role at all in court discussions', he wrote, demoralized by his powerlessness and by the corruption of the court. The closer he got to the throne, the clearer he saw the true nature of power when justice goes astray:

It was a time when the powerful indulged in murder and plunder...
The military used up the tax grain in the stores... the imperial fighting cocks had to be fed.
Many warnings could have been obtained from history about why a dynasty falls...

Beset by a cycle of worsening weather, economic decline and social unrest, the mood in the nation was changing. Where the Brilliant Emperor had once been a model of enlightened rule, he was now in his sixties and had become negligent. Infatuated with his concubine Yang Guifei, he rewarded her family and promoted corrupt ministers. Throughout Chinese history, the problem has been the same. The country is so big that if its rulers lose their grip, things fall apart.

Corruption and favouritism were widespread, and Du Fu made them the subject of brilliantly observed critiques. In one from 753 he imagines a spring outing at Winding River Park in Xi'an, the detail so vivid and circumstantial one may wonder whether he was present as a minor functionary. He conjures fabulous images of a *déjeuner sur l'herbe*, his poetry replete with beautiful ladies, ornate tents and brocade carpets. In one, the sister of Yang Guifei herself is among those picnicking on rare delicacies – camel hump soup, slivers of raw fish eaten with ivory chopsticks. The poem ends with an ominous warning, the old adage that a divine ruler's godlike gaze could burn up the unwary onlooker:

Where power is all-surpassing, fingers may be burned.
Take care, draw no closer to His Excellency's glare.

It was around this time that Du Fu had a strange and prophetic experience, what almost sounds like a sudden seizure (perhaps a clue to his sometimes visionary out-of-body poems?). On a light-hearted trip with friends to the Wild Goose temple, he climbed to the top of the pagoda and looked out across the great city at sunset to the palaces and the Wei river beyond, only to have a kind of fit. The river disappeared, the imperial city crumbled and dissolved in a miasma, 'and the wild geese flew away'.

It was a forecast of things to come. The empire was going into crisis, frontier wars had led to higher taxes, and mass conscription hit the poor. In his own life, too, things did not look up. His hopes of meaningful employment were dashed when he was offered a job as a district officer whose chief duty was to judge and whip draft evaders and tax cheats. He declined the offer and was shunted off to look after the arms stores. At that point in autumn 755, with social unrest growing, the nation was hit by rains and floods which lasted more than sixty days, leaving half the capital under water. His poems take on a new tone, describing the prolonged rains and the human suffering:

> *rains hiss-hiss, the cold comes early; since the start of autumn not once have we seen the sun; this earth of ours is waterlogged and fouled – when will it ever dry?*

As food ran out in the city Du Fu sent his family into the countryside northeast of Chang'an to the village of Fengxian where one of his wife's family was a magistrate. There at least they would be safe.

7
The Road to Fengxian

'I am ashamed to call myself a father'

Pucheng, today's Fengxian, lies a hundred miles north-east of Xi'an. It is essentially a modern town; almost nothing survives from earlier history. I travelled out there on a bleak day of rain and low cloud. In the centre near the county office is the Confucian temple; it was smashed in the Cultural Revolution and the nondescript statue of the Master was only reinstalled in 1997. But behind the temple there's an attractive courtyard with a forest of inscribed pillars, a prayer hall, and beyond that a tall brick pagoda. In a columned portico there's a pile of broken stonework with a big fragment of a Qing dynasty stele inscribed: 'Former Residence of Du Fu', but the true site of the family home, if it was ever known, has been long since lost. The municipality is making up for this with a brand new Du Fu memorial hall, its shiny black marble foundation stele recently inaugurated by local dignitaries. It's an invention, of course, of a kind you'll find everywhere nowadays in China, but he *was* here.

The Confucian temple at Pucheng.

And his spirit is still here in the bleak countryside, where with a little sympathetic imagination we can touch on one of his most memorable and tragic moments. After months apart and famine reaching across a rain-swept landscape, he gets leave to visit the family. It's December and the weather is freezing:

500 Words on the Road to Fengxian

At the years ending… a bitter wind scours the high ridges.
I set out a lone traveller at midnight…
Fingers too cold to tie my broken belt.
At dawn I passed the Imperial Palace
Here at the hot springs the emperor entertains his court
And music echoes around the hills.
Only the rich and powerful may bathe here,
But the silk they wear was woven by poor people,
Women whose husbands are beaten for their taxes.
The Halls are full of ladies as fair as goddesses
The scent of perfume moves with each captivating figure
Clothed in the warm furs of sable,
Entertained with the finest music, pipes and strings…
Fed with camel hump soup and oranges ripened in the frost.
Behind the red lacquered gates, wine is left to sour, meat to rot.
Outside the gates lie the bones of the frozen and the starveds….
When I returned home wailing rose in the house
My infant child had died of hunger.
Why should I hold back my grief
When even the neighbours in the village are crying for us?
I am ashamed of being a father;
So poor that I caused my son to die for lack of food.
How could I know that the autumn harvest
Still could not save the poor from disaster?
And I am one of the privileged:
If my life is so bitter
Then how much worse is the life of the common people?

The death of his boy he never forgot. In the very last poem he wrote, lying dying on a boat near Lake Dongting, he would compare himself to the ill-fated poet and statesman Pan Yue, 'alike in burying a child who died young'. Artfully constructed as it is, the reader may be tempted to think the poem has a rawness of feeling that sounds as if it was written as an immediate reaction while still in the midst of grief and shame. It's as if in his borrowed house in the village, he had sat down in a room, or gone out to walk in the fields, singing or chanting the song, and then sitting down with his old leather arm rest, getting out his brushes, wetting his ink block, and in his brush strokes giving order to the chaos swirling around him, both in the outside world, and in his mind. The poem is held up as an example of his 'sincerity', but that is perhaps to underestimate his artfulness. Du Fu by now was a very accomplished poet, and we should be careful not to identify his 'writing from the heart' with the real experience of writing such a poem.

The detail is mesmerizing in its immediacy. But one might ask, how autobiographical is it? Does the road, for example, actually lead that way past the hot springs to Fengxian? Or has he put the two together to make the bigger point, the collision between rich and poor, the personal and the political? How much is this a brilliant though heartfelt construct? Looking at the map, from the flooded south of Chang'an, the quarter of poor civil servants like him, the road's natural route does indeed lead north-west towards the Wei River past the Huaqing Palace, and across the river beyond Weinan. It sounds real; the impulse to put these ideas together in one bold visionary outpouring. Perhaps it is a true story. After the heart pounding, brain fogging, the grief and shame, recollecting the emotion with a measure of tranquillity and giving them order by putting brush to paper?

8

The War of An Lushan

'The state is destroyed'

On 16 December 755, within weeks, perhaps even days, of arriving at the village, Du Fu's world changed for ever. The great rebellion of An Lushan began. A renegade Turkic general, son of a Sogdian shamaness, and a man favoured by the emperor, as Du Fu said, with 'an abundance of grace', An Lushan marched on the capital from North China with a quarter of a million men. On 8 January he crossed the Yellow River, defeated the imperial armies and captured the eastern capital Luoyang. On 5 February An Lushan declared himself emperor of the new 'Great Yan dynasty'. In Xi'an, the court was seized with panic. Loyal imperial generals had prepared a strong defence line at the Tong pass on the road to Xi'an, but the leaders were removed from power and executed by a court faction, which then took the disastrous decision to come down into the plain and attack the rebels. There, on 7 July, in a huge, pitched battle, they were defeated. The emperor and his family and their staff then decided to abandon Xi'an and flee over the mountains into Sichuan. On the way, at Mawei post station, the imperial guard assassinated the councillors whom they blamed for bringing on the disaster, but also demanded the death of the imperial concubine Yang Guifei. Grief-stricken, the emperor gave her up and saw her strangled with a silken cloth – a never-to-be-forgotten scene immortalized in the poet Bai Juyi's 'Song of Everlasting Sorrow'.

Du Fu and his young family were swept up in these disasters, just one family among the millions who fled the armies. As the rebels closed in on the capital in July 756, they took to the road again, moving north from Fengxian, going from place to place, reduced to taking charity just to survive. It would become a way of life.

Ballad of Pengya Road

I remember when we first fled the rebels,
hurrying north over dangerous trails;
night deepened on Pengya Road.
The whole family trudging endlessly
begging without shame from the people we met.
Not a single traveller came the other way.
My little girl bit me in her hunger
And fearful that wolves or tigers would hear her cries
I hugged her to my chest, muffling her mouth.
But still she struggled free and just cried more.
Ten days we went holding hands, half in rain and thunder,
Through mud and slime we pulled each other on,
No escaping the rain …
Eating wild berries, sheltering under trees
Wading through water, searching the horizon for a wisp of smoke
That might lead us to a safe shelter….

Has any poet so urgently recorded what it feels like to be a refugee, fleeing for your life? The war was the turning point in Du Fu's life, and the great divide in his poetry. Now he knew what it meant to be, as Shakespeare would put it, 'a poor naked unaccommodated man'. It is the realism of these poems which is so striking to the modern reader. He gives voice to the poor and downtrodden: the mother who has lost her sons; the refugee whose husband has abandoned her and whose brothers have all been killed; the old man coming home to his destroyed village to find his mother buried in a 'ditch of a grave'. These are voices that had never been heard before in any literature, but voices we hear in our living rooms today, for example in

An Lushan: an imaginary portrait of China's bogeyman.

the Ukrainian tragedy, where suffering civilians speak to the cameras directly, harrowed faces in devastated apartment blocks in Mariupol or Kherson telling of bombing, rape and murder. 'Everywhere I look,' Du Fu wrote, 'I see the sorrow of human existence'.

He seems to have understood the implications of this for his career as a poet, for the bulk of his surviving poetry (which, as we have seen, he edited and preserved) comes from after this time. In other words, he edited his literary work in this way because he knew that this was when he had found the voice. 'Literature,' as the poet Bai Juyi wrote later, 'should be written to accord with the times'. And for Du Fu the act of writing now had become not only a consolation, but a necessity: 'without poetry what would I be?'

The twists and turns of Du Fu's life take some piecing together here, but what we know is this: in summer 756 the capital fell to An Lushan's army. Du Fu describes this awful moment in his poem, 'Back Then In'. Here are the opening lines of thirty-three couplets (the wooden tablets are the spirit plaques of the deceased Tang rulers in the ancestral shrines):

Back then in those days of the western capital
The Hu came, filling the crimson palace.
In the middle of the night they burned the nine temples,
The river of stars turned red.
The breaking tiles flew for ten leagues,
The tassled curtains were everywhere in the sky.
My heart depressed pities the wooden tablets,
One by one ashes in the mournful wind.
At twilight the armoured cavalry formed lines,
In clear dawn light their brocade trappings scattered
Rebel officials showed their betrayal,
Congratulating each other on their success.
At this time the imperial consorts were massacred
In succession, becoming piles of dirt
Behind palace doors the jade throne fell...

Thousands of citizens were killed; markets, houses and shops looted; and the accumulated wealth of the Silk Road, the warehouses of the Sogdian merchants, all went up in smoke. Writing at the time, Du Fu conveys the panic and confusion in hallucinatory imagery, depicting the aftermath of the rebels' arrival in the capital as thousands of refugees blocked the roads, accompanied by sinister omens of disaster:

White headed crows shrieking over Chang'an city walls
Circling in the night, cawing above Greeting Autumn Gate
Then they turn on the homes of the people, pecking at the great mansions,
Mansions where high officials scramble to flee the barbarians…

In one powerful vignette, he meets a dishevelled royal prince standing weeping by the roadside, still wearing his insignia of rank:

How pathetic – a costly disc of green coral at his waist
I ask but he won't tell me his name or surname,
Says only that he is worn out and in trouble, begs me to make him my servant.

With panic all around them, the conversation is brief:

I can't talk for long here at the crossroads, there are informers everywhere.
Last night the winds blew rank with the smell of blood:
From the east camels [of An Lushan's army] crowding into the old capital.

Du Fu gives the young man the news. The emperor has gone in the night, fled south to the Uighurs who have sworn to help. There may still be hope:

Take care – say nothing of our conversation –
I'm sorry for you prince, take care and do nothing rash
There are still auspicious signs over the imperial graves…

The emperor and his court had fled, but when Du Fu tried to join them he was captured on the road by the rebels. Too lowly to warrant execution, he was taken as a captive back to the capital, once more separated from his family. Among the poems he wrote then were famous verses to his wife, using language conventionally used of a courtesan but describing a beloved wife, it has been claimed, for the first time in Chinese poetry:

The moon shines in Fuzhou tonight,
in her chamber, she watches alone.
Her cloud-like hair is sweet with mist,
Her jade arms cold in the clear moonlight.
When shall we lean in the empty window,
together in brightness, our tears dried up?

Who was Du Fu's wife? It was rare for writers to talk about their wives. We know she was Madame Yang, daughter of Yang Yi, a minister in the court. As a member of the Office of National Granaries, Yang held an important post responsible for the distribution of central government grain stores and revenues. Du Fu married Madame Yang when he was around forty, and unlike many of his contemporaries, does not seem to have taken further wives or concubines. When she died we don't know, but she outlived her husband, bringing up their children.

Du Fu didn't write much poetry about his wife early on, and it is only from late 755, when the war began, that he started to describe the family in detail. 'Moonlit Night' is much admired today for its expression of love and separation, more realistic it is said than anything in Chinese literature before him. But are we entitled to imagine anything more? Cloud-like hair and jade-smooth skin are conventional poetic descriptions, though we assume she was physically attractive in his eyes. Poems written here and elsewhere (especially in Chengdu) portray her as a loving mother, teaching her children and improvising a chess board out of paper. But what she was really like we don't know. Husband and wife clearly wrote to each other regularly when apart, as they frequently were. Did she complain about his absences? Get fed up with his illnesses, his bouts of depression and his at times self-pitying attitude? She certainly seems steadfastly loyal, courageous and very resourceful. But how did she respond to their disasters? As the daughter of a high-ranking minister, did she blame her husband for failing the family? And was Du Fu ashamed of the difficult life he gave his long-suffering wife, who, as the saying went, was reduced to the point of being 'a beggar living off funeral offerings'? His Fengxian poem suggests this was the case.

Du Fu's poem 'Journey to the North' gives us a few answers. In it, he comes home with gifts of face powder and mascara, a quilt and hangings, and 'my thin wife's face glowed again'. As for the kids, his favourite son, whom he nicknamed 'Pony Boy', is now a scruffy, undernourished urchin:

The boy I've spoiled all his life
Is so hungry his face is paler than snow
Now he sees Dad and turns away to cry;
Dirty and grimy, no socks upon his feet

And also from 'Journey to the North' there is foreboding about the road ahead:

I've come home alive and I'm with my children
Soon I'll forget pangs of hunger and thirst.
Now I'm back home I can relax for a while.
But what can I say about our lives in the future?

Du Fu spent that winter and the following spring confined in the rebel-occupied capital, living for a time in Great Cloud (Dayun) monastery, whose abbot he had befriended – 'my arm-in-arm companion'. For a time, William Hung conjectures, he was forced by the rebels to labour as a porter pulling carts; hard for a man who, though a fit young horseman in his prime, was now in his forties and increasingly dogged by bad health, asthma and recurrent bouts of malaria. Thoughts of his own mortality now come thick and fast in his verse: the destruction of the state, as well as the resilience and patience of the people.

It was at this time that Du Fu wrote one of his most celebrated poems. The specific occasion was probably a walk Du Fu says he made 'furtively' by the lake in the city's deserted Serpentine Park, past the abandoned waterside palaces. The opening line of five stark syllables – *guo po shan-he zai* – is perhaps the most famous in Chinese literature:

The state is destroyed, but the country remains.
In the city in spring, grass and weeds grow everywhere
Grieving for the times, even the blossom sheds tears,
Hating the separation birds startle the heart
Beacon fires have been burning for three months now.
A letter from home would be worth ten thousand in gold...
Scratching my head, my white hair is getting thinner:
soon it won't hold a hairpin.

The title 'Spring Scene' invites a simple expectation. We think of what spring has always meant in Chinese culture, with the glorious spectacle of the spring blossom. Now the City of Peace is half abandoned, but the natural world still endures, and every year spring renews itself, whatever the fate of humankind. But now, he imagines, even nature is not indifferent to human suffering, the new buds themselves seeming to shed tears. Then the camera – as it were – opens wide to human affairs, panning across a country enveloped in war, the beacon fires carrying a sense of unremitting warfare. Then finally the poem moves from the political to the personal ('what wouldn't I give for a letter from my wife!'). And then the wry and poignant final line; though only in his late forties, Du Fu is conscious of his declining health, how he now looks like an old person: 'my hair is so thin it won't hold a hairpin' (the pin that Chinese males used to hold up their hair in a bun).

This poem has had a huge resonance in Chinese literature through the ages. We think of Li Qingzhao joining panic-stricken refugees flooding south after the fall of Kaifeng in 1127 with her precious scrolls of Du Fu's poetry; or Zheng Yunduan echoing him in her heartbreaking verses in besieged Suzhou at the fall of the Yuan; or Fang Weiyi resorting to poetry in the last days of the Ming amid flames of revolt and the Manchu invasion. (And how interesting to note that these great poets are all women.) Later, amid the horrors of the Taiping War, Zheng Zhen, whom many think the greatest poet of modern China, wrote dense poems modelled on Du Fu, and in a lull in the savagery journeyed from Guizhou all the way up to Chengdu to meditate at the site of Du Fu's cottage – a place of pilgrimage of greater spiritual significance to him than any temple.

Du Fu gave these later poets a way of seeing, a faith in a moral order, and empathy with suffering people. Poets, he thought, should bear witness to their times. 'Spring Scene' in particular is known by all Chinese people today. On YouTube there is a video of Li Tien, an American-Chinese man, reading it aloud at the Midland Michigan Poetry Club in 2011. Li had been a child during the horrors of the Japanese occupation and describes seeing the famous opening line of Du Fu's poem daubed on the wall of a ruined building in his devastated hometown: *The state is destroyed, but the country remains*. He reads the poem in Chinese and then explains: 'I did not choose this poem. The poem chose me.'

9

West to Qinzhou

'Everywhere I look, the sorrow of human existence'

The war lasted more than seven years and would be a great divide in Chinese history. Though An Lushan himself was assassinated in January 757, murdered by his own son, the revolt continued, devastating much of central China. The imperial armies fought back, recruiting Arab, Uighur and Sogdian mercenaries, and at one point deployed nine battle groups to attack the rebel base. But the collapse of the state, and the order and protection it afforded to the people, was apparent everywhere. The state was indeed broken, with rebel groups rampaging across the regions. The Tang dynasty had over a century still to run, but it never fully recovered.

'In this vast whirling chaos there is no end to the sorrow,' Du Fu wrote. The Chinese word he uses to describe the war, *luan,* meaning chaos, conveys the nightmare of social instability that now swept the country. Despite An Lushan's death, horrendous violence continued, with pogroms of foreign communities, the sacking of cities and civilian massacres. Daily life was turned upside down: there were food shortages everywhere, prices shot up, and with rice at 'ten thousand per *tou*', starvation stalked the land. In the stories told by Tai Fu we hear of the constant danger of bandits on roads and rivers, the killing of loyal prefects and magistrates and their families, massacres of entire villages. Amid the tide of war, he describes passing oxcarts on the roads carrying the dead, and meeting a flautist from the royal orchestra hiding in a cave in the mountains. The ideal of Chinese civilization was stripped bare.

According to the Tang censuses, thirty-six million people were lost during this time, victims of war, famine, or displaced as refugees over the seven years until February 763. Some modern historians have scaled this down to thirteen million dead, but either way, this was the worst war in history at that point, and is still today one of the worst. Among the millions who never returned was Du Fu, he and his starving family driven from place to place as refugees. Before the modern era surely no artist has so faithfully recorded the everyday experience of the sufferings of common humanity during a devastating war.

The war was a turning point for Du Fu in both his life and his art. His tendency, already conspicuous in his poetry, towards social commentary – dealing with war, taxation, corruption, the consumption and indolence of the rich and powerful – was now a clear voice. Freed from the need to please those in power, from here on Du Fu recorded what happened to him, obsessively describing his own experience. It is hard to think of such an intimate autobiographical account of a person's life anywhere in the world before him.

Du Fu spent that winter and spring 756 in the devastated capital Chang'an under rebel occupation, suffering from malaria and asthma ('my sick lungs'). Meanwhile, the new emperor Suzong regrouped his forces to launch a counter-attack from his base at Lingzhou on the Yellow River 300 miles north-west of Chang'an, and the capital was retaken. This triumph was followed by a settling of scores. Like the poet Wang Wei, Du Fu was at first accused of being a collaborator but was eventually set free and reinstated in the service of Suzong back in Chang'an. He was appointed a 'Left Reminder', a remonstrance official whose duties were to inform His Majesty of errors in official documents, whether in content or style. He was pleased at this recognition of his literary skills. It was the apex, such as it was, of his official career.

But nothing was straightforward with Du Fu. In autumn 757 he infuriated the emperor by criticizing him and speaking up for a loyal general who had been defeated by the rebels. He was placed under arrest and put on trial, only for the judges to conclude that, although 'too free with his words', Du Fu had been faithful to his duties. He was eventually pardoned and allowed time off to return to Qiang village in Fuzhou where his wife and children were now staying. After an absence of over a year, the family were reunited, and the three poems he wrote celebrating his return, translated here by Burton Watson, are among the most revealing about his relations with his wife.

My wife amazed to see me alive,
Recovers from her astonishment, wipes away tears.
A world in chaos, buffeted, tumbled,
By sheerest chance I've managed to make it back.
Faces of the neighbours crowd the wall;
pitying, they add their sighs and exclamations.
As night deepens, we bring out candles,
Face one another as though in a dream

In the second poem Du Fu describes their children, especially his younger son:

Along in years, barely managing to stay alive,
I came home to find pleasures few.
My dear boy won't let go of my knees,
Afraid I'll go off and leave him again

The third poem gives a fascinating insight into the actual practice of poetry. As they shoo the chickens away, there's a knock at the door:

Four or five village elders
Come to ask about my long absence, my long trip home.
Each carries something in his hand;

From tilted casks, muddy wine, and clear,
Profuse apologies for the wine's poor flavour:
'No one these days to work the millet fields,
Wars and uprisings that never end,
All the young ones off to the eastern campaign'

Then a lovely moment in the candlelit hut as the poet, in gratitude for the villagers' poor gift of home-made rice wine, 'muddy' with sediment, offers in return to give them the only thing he can offer in return – a poem:

I ask if I may sing them a song,
Sign of my deep gratitude in these troublesome times.
Song ended, I gaze upwards with a sigh,
From those on all four sides, tears streaming down.

It's a touching scene of the family and the village elders in the little candlelit hut; and one of Du Fu's numerous references to the singing of poetry. We can only assume here that he sings one of his own poems. The word used in Chinese for 'sing them a song' is *ge*, and the song ending is also *ge*; the first a verb, the second a noun. When poets talk about *ge*, it means that they are singing or reciting rhythmically, often striking a bowl or the table for percussion. Classical Chinese poetry was usually sung.

Back with his family, Du Fu digs and plants his garden, watering the fields and growing food, while reflecting on the disastrous rupture the war caused not only in the state but in people's lives. In one poem he gives powerful voice to an (imagined?) poor man with no family left: 'a man with no family to take leave of: how can you call me a proper human being?' The village is wrecked: 'silence and desolation, fields and sheds mere masses of pigweed and bramble ... my village had a hundred households or more – now in these troubled times the people are scattered east and west'.

Du Fu returned to court in spring 758, still taking his duties very seriously. He tells us in one poem that he worked all day and through the night to finish one memorial to the emperor. But his honesty and obstinacy rubbed people up the wrong way; a friend advised him to 'remonstrate less frequently'. He was soon drinking too much: 'I don't care if people drop me: I really don't fit in this world'. In the summer he was demoted, sent off to Huazhou, 75 miles east of Xi'an, where he was employed as a local government functionary.

Huazhou lay on the old road back to Luoyang, today's G310, near to the sacred mountain Huashan and its bustling pilgrim town. As we have seen, it was a road he knew well from his youthful journeying to the capital, but the town was culturally desolate, and he was stuck in a dead-end job, responsible for schools, exams, temples and ceremonial occasions. 'I wanted to scream,' he wrote, 'especially as more and more papers piled up on my desk'. It was during this time that he made a trip to Luoyang on government business and seems to have taken the opportunity to revisit the family estate at Tulou near Luoyang, the 'lost domain' that haunted him; but he was shocked by how unfamiliar the war-ravaged gardens and paths appeared: 'in the interim they have become a battlefield – I can't even find my rickety gate.' He would never see his old home again.

In 759 the imperial armies suffered another heavy defeat. In the aftermath Du Fu wrote a famous poem on the arrival of a recruiting sergeant with a press gang one night when the poet was staying at an inn on government business at Shihao – 'Stone Moat village' – in Henan (that he is so precise about the place surely lets us know that this is a real scene he had observed himself). As the soldiers barge into the inn, an old man frantically scrambles over the compound wall to escape. Later the poet has a conversation with a woman in the inn who has heard by letter from her son that his two brothers have been killed in battle with the rebels:

Late that night no more sound of people talking
But I thought I heard weeping and muffled sobs.
At dawn when I set out once more,
Only the old man to see me off

Finally, in late autumn 759, he had had enough: 'I'm getting on for fifty now,' he wrote. 'I'm free to stop working as an official. Why force myself to take on trivial tasks?' He resigned his official post, packed what belongings the family had, and left. Till now he had always hoped to get back to the capital, and his motive for abandoning that hope is usually said to have simply been poverty and famine. This may have been so, compounded by the fact that his career had hit rock bottom. But he also wanted to protect his family. Perhaps he hoped to find security with family members or friends beyond the mountains in Sichuan. The family headed back towards the capital with the intention of continuing further west. They were a small gaggle of people, with their family servants and their belongings in a cart drawn by his old horse. Du Fu had quite a large extended family, including brothers, half-brothers and sisters, with all of whom he tried to keep in touch by letter, and travelling with him now was a younger half-brother. We shouldn't underestimate how brave they were to take this leap, but maybe the alternative was starvation. They travelled up the valley of the Wei River, leaving the capital behind them. He would never see it again. They travelled on over Dragon Massif, the escarpment between the central plain of Shaanxi, and the mountainous uplands to the west, stopping for a short time in the region of Qinzhou, today's Tianshui, where the landscape opens out on the old Silk Road through Gansu to the west.

10

Maijishan: Haystack Mountain

'So huge the compass of heaven and earth, so long the road I travel'

Thirty miles south-east of Qinzhou is Maijishan, magical and mysterious, and still pretty much untouched. Today it's reachable by car or local bus from Tianshui, but up until the 1950s it was virtually unknown to outsiders, so remote that it was described by none of the early western writers on China. It is absolutely spectacular – another world from the glitz of modern China.

Close Encounters: the majestic setting of Maijishan.

Buddhist statuary on Maijishan.

A short way off the main track of the Silk Road towards Central Asia, its name means 'Haystack Mountain'. It is a giant brown sandstone pyramid rising abruptly above the forest, its crumbling terraces from a distance looking like eroded natural striations. Its pock-marked cliffs probably once sheltered an ancient Daoist retreat amid these rugged pine-clad hills, then it became a home to Buddhist hermits who established a small monastery here, which a sixth-century writer thought evoked Sumeru, the Buddhist holy mountain, the mythical axis of the universe. Another Chinese transplant from India, nearly 200 cave shrines survive from its heyday in the early fifth century through the boom time of the sixth, carved into the side of the great red sandstone cliff which rises abruptly out of the forests.

Crammed with sculptures and murals, many still covered with paint, today the caves are accessible by teetering wooden walkways over vertiginous drops, so remote that their murals and still intact statuary were only examined and mapped in the 1950s and photographed in 1958. As the expedition diarist the young Romila Thapar wrote, 'the rock of Maijishan was most inspiring from a distance, especially in the late afternoon with rain clouds behind it surrounded by the hills, standing out from them with its red-brown surface. From the courtyard on nights when there was a moon, the East Facade resembled the Shikara of an Indian temple drawn in the nineteenth century, the colossal T'ang Buddhas on the facade giving it an atmosphere of romantic discovery'.

Maijishan had its last heyday in the Ming and Qing dynasties, but it then sank into oblivion, with just 'Elder Wang' – an eighty-year-old monk, living there as its guardian until 1958 – the last living connection with that long and marvellous history.

As we know, Du Fu was often drawn to Buddhist and Daoist monasteries, both for spiritual knowledge and for temporary food and accommodation. Here at Maijishan he met up again with his friend Abbot Zan, once head of the Dayun temple in the capital, whom Du Fu tells us in a note attached to one of his poems had also been banished to Qinzhou and, 'his face now gaunt and lined with care', was living in exile out here in Gansu. 'In this strange place I came across my old friend, and with newfound delight poured out my feelings'.

Du Fu and his family seem to have stayed in the area for several weeks, perhaps for a time at the temple below the cliff with its guesthouse and outbuildings. Looking from the upper terraces of the caves, rows of hills stretch to the horizon seamed with snow in winter; undulating ranges covered with pine forests, triangular pinnacles stretching to the horizon.

MOUNTAIN TEMPLE

Few monks remain in the wilderness temple,
a tiny track goes high to its mountain garden.
A musk-deer sleeps among stones and bamboo,
Parrots peck at golden peaches.
A tangle of rock allows a person to pass,
on the hanging cliff cells are securely set.
In the highest precincts, evening in the tiered tower,
From a hundred li I could make out
a strand of autumn hair.

This is where the family found themselves in winter 759. Conditions were grim. It was bitterly cold, for a time cut off by snow: 'Nothing on the stove,' he despaired. 'At dawn the well is frozen: I've no long coat and at night my bed is so cold.' No rural idyll, then; life was very tough, basic subsistence living for the family. But he seems to have hoped at one stage to build a house near Qinzhou and to live there permanently ('though I haven't told the kids yet').

In the event Du Fu spent just six weeks in the region. Sixty poems survive, including a series entitled 'Twenty Varied

'Seeing for a hundred miles' – the view from Maijishan.

Qinzhou verses'. Many are shot through with the harsh beauty of the landscape. For the modern visitor it is a good base for travels in the mountains to find the places he describes. The Nanguo temple lies on the north hill of Mount Huyin, a mile or so from the town, with its 'north flowing spring' and ancient cypress trees. Inside the temple Du Fu's Qinzhou poems are carved on a huge stone stele. Then there is the landscape to the south near Chengzhou, with its 'fathomless' pool and deep-cut gorge. Later antiquarians picked over his track here, poems in hand, and nineteenth-century gazetteers, bursting with local patriotism, enthusiastically identified the sites of 'Du Fu's Temple', 'Du Fu's Thatched Hut', the Village Spring, and 'Du Fu's Tree', all of which are still there today.

The family were not the only refugees there. With the fall of the capital, many people had fled westwards, and among Du Fu's chance encounters with others carried there with the wrack of war was a noblewoman fallen on hard times, whom in verses perhaps from this time he describes meeting in one of the many lonely valleys in the wooded hinterland of

Qinzhou. The poem, 'Lovely Lady', speaks for itself, beginning like a timeless popular song:

Lovely lady, fairest of the time,
Hiding away in an empty valley;
Daughter of a good house, she said,
Fallen now among the grasses of the wood.
'There was tumult and death within the passes then;
my brothers old and young all killed.
Office, position – what help were they?
I couldn't even gather up my brothers' bones!
The world despises you when your luck is down;
All I had went with the turn of the flame.
My husband was a fickle fellow,
His new girls as fair as jade.
Blossoms that close at dusk keep faith with the hour,
Mandarin ducks will not rest apart;
But he could only see the new one laughing,
Never hear the former one's tears.'
Within the mountain the stream runs clear;
Out of the mountain it turns to mud.
Her maid returns from selling a pearl,
Braids vines to mend their roof of thatch.
The lady picks a flower but does not put it in her hair,
Gathers juniper berries, sometimes a handful.
When the sky is cold, in thin azure sleeves,
At dusk she stands leaning by the tall bamboo

It has been suggested that Du Fu artfully invented the beautiful woman, that the poem is purely allegorical. But like others among his ballads, the specifics sound circumstantial and William Hung and Eva Chou, among others, think that she must have been a real person. Fleeing with her household servants, perhaps the 'lovely lady' has sold off her belongings on the way, and

'Daughter of a good house'.

now hasn't even enough clothes for the cold. It snows heavily in Qinzhou in the winter, and she's sleeping in the most basic peasant's hovel. In this tide of suffering and death, many people like her had fled west from the capital; from poor conscripts to old noble families, human bonds broken and lives trashed.

11

The Journey South: From Chestnut Station to White Sands

'If I die . . .'

Though the family had escaped the capital, the war caught up with Du Fu again. As autumn deepened, local rebel forces swept west to Qinzhou and again a tide of refugees took to the road.

Autumn on the way to Chestnut Station.

Still desperate for food and in fear of their lives, the family decided to leave the Qinzhou region and to head further south. In late 759 he said an affectionate goodbye to Abbot Zan and set off, at times travelling by night like a journey in a dark fairy tale:

At midnight I set off by wagon,
watering my horse in cold embankment streams
So huge the compass of heaven and earth
So long the road I travel…
Cold skies thick with frost and snow,
But we travellers must keep moving.
At dawn I set off from Red Valley station,
Steep perilous roads from this point on,
A jumble of stones, no other cart track to follow –
I've already greased the axles well.
In the deep mountains a strong wind makes the going harder.
Come nightfall my little ones are hungry,
Spirits flag, village so far off.
We can see smoke but how to get there?

He mocked himself for his optimistic fantasies that things would be better in Tonggu, that there would be plentiful food. 'I'm old, stupid, listless, I can't seem to make any plans for my life. There's nothing to eat so I ask after the "Happy Land"' (the land of plenty the starving peasants dream of in the *Book of Odes*).

They say the weather there's like a bracing autumn
Grass and trees not yet yellowed or stripped,
Waters more wonderful still
Chestnut Pavilion – a most auspicious name!
Surely rich farmlands must surround it,
Lots of wild yams to fill the belly,
honeycombs in the cliffs easy to gather…
True there's the hardships of a long journey,
but hopefully I'll find there what I've always longed for

Plankway, Gansu, 1910: 'our perilous path teetering along the middle of a cliff face... why did I put my wife and children through this?'.

The family had been on the edge of starvation for weeks. Their lack of food now is a constant theme in his writing, and his children seem never free of the ache of hunger. Always there are hints of relentless pressure, sudden starts, journeys at night. It was about 130 miles by a circuitous route on local tracks, crossing the Western Han River, but there was a delay after the horse pulling their cart hurt its leg crossing the river in Tietang Gorge. Perhaps his lovely tribute to his horse ('My Sick Horse') was written around this time:

It's a long time since I first rode you
Far along the frontier and deep in winter.
You have toiled hard in this world all your life.
I grieve now over your age and your illness.
There's nothing special about your appearance;
But your good temperament and loyal service have been constant.
The noble significance of a human creature is touching
And worthy of a sad song.

They were now refugees pure and simple, passing through impoverished villages where 'the village lanes for my sake put on the face of pity'. To make things worse, the weather turned:

Mountains on all sides, high winds, canyon waters swift;
Cold rain sloshes down, bare trees soaked
Yellow mugwort over town walls, clouds that never lift,
Why has my life brought me to this forsaken valley?

It was nearly a month before they got to Tonggu. Today you can do the journey in a couple of hours or so by car or by local bus along the modern G316. The untouched landscape off the beaten track (as he said) is still splendid, with deep forests of pine. At the end of the year, they reached Chestnut Station, a village named after a Tang government rest house just beyond Tonggu. Here he stayed for two months at the Fa Jing monastery. Again the landmarks are still pointed out today: 'Du Fu's Thatched House' and a Du Fu memorial hall complete with a weathered statue of the poet.

But it turned out there was no security at Chestnut Station. In freezing weather the month's stay was a truly miserable time for the family. He built a hut at the foot of Phoenix Mountain at the mouth of Fei Long Gorge, where he 'climbed mountains with thin clothes, chapped face and frostbitten hands' to collect acorns that the family could peel, boil, mash and eat.

'The great river stirred before me, surging as broad as a dark sea' – Du Fu at the Shuihui crossing: one of a cycle painted in 1959 by Lu Yanshao.

It was here in late 759, in desperate circumstances, that he wrote the famous cycle 'Seven Songs of Tonggu'. These poems have been much commented on, and frequently imitated, though there has been, and still is, argument over what Du Fu was actually trying to do with them. Each of the seven songs begins with a repetition, in the manner of a ballad. Here are the opening lines of the first four songs (in the first line of verse one, Zimei is Du Fu's courtesy name, the name given to a young man when he turns twenty):

Verse one: I'm a sojourner, a sojourner, Zimei is my name...
Verse two: I've got a hoe, a hoe, long handle of white wood...
Verse three: I've got brothers, younger brothers, living far far away...
Verse four: I've got a sister, little sister, living in Zhongji...

In each song or stanza, the middle four lines tell a story, then each ends with a repeating lament, a rhyming couplet beginning with *wu hu* ('alas alack'), whose first line numbers the song's place in the series, and whose second line gives the payoff, which we might compare with what Lorca memorably calls the *duende*, the flood of emotion inspired by poetry, music or art which brings laughter or tears:

Wu hu, I sing my first song, a song already full of pain
And a mournful wind comes from the sky to blow me on again

And so on for the seven songs. It is agreed by commentators that Du Fu was trying something experimental here, breaking out of the usual form of the ballad tradition. The feel is of an old-fashioned song, with the repeated use of the words *wu hu*, 'alas alack'. There is a surviving tradition of singing these songs today which is very distinctive, dramatically different from the way of singing other Tang poetry. With sharp, percussive, bitten-off opening lines, then at the end a slow dying fall with voice vibrato (suggesting, to the western ear, perhaps an unaccompanied Delta Blues, especially in the passionate forceful singing style).

How far back this tradition goes is not known, but there are clues to his literary models. The first song begins in the same way as an old poem in the *Shijing*, the *Classic of Poetry*, and echoes a number of early traditional ballads, the 'Nine Songs' and the famous 'Eighteen Verses of a Nomad Flute' attributed to the fourth-century female composer and poet Cai Wenji. But today's singers especially cite as Du Fu's influence *Si Chou Shi*,

Sword Gate, leading down into the Chengdu Plain.

'Four Sorrows', by the Han dynasty scientist and poet Zhang Heng. So, Du Fu was evidently explicitly setting himself in that tradition of folk lament. For the structure of the songs, we might make a distant analogy with the cumulative song in the European tradition, as in traditional English folk song where the refrain is repeated:

I'll sing you one, O
Green grow the rushes O!
What is your one, O?
One is one and all alone
And ever more shall be so
I'll sing you two, O…

And so on to twelve. In European literature these take different forms as children's songs or teaching songs, but though there are examples of the cumulative song in the Ming, the form doesn't seem to be known earlier as a feature of Chinese poetry. It is tempting, though, to imagine Du Fu and his family with their horse and cart, struggling on, shivering with fear, cold and hunger, and as he tells us, singing popular songs with their simple repetitions to keep spirits up, which then triggered his own darker poems, throwing in a balladeer's tricks we might see in modern times in folk song or blues:

If I die here how will you find my bones?

Another element of the 'Seven Songs' which might be seen to bring them into the orbit of traditional ballads and fairy tales is the introduction of the strange and magical, monsters and ogres. In the sixth stanza, Du Fu brings in not the bloodthirsty giant but a dragon and serpents:

In the south lives a dragon in a mountain pool
Where old trees dark and lush, touch limb to bending limb
When leaves yellow and fall, he goes to his winter sleep…
And from the east come serpents to play on the waters there.
Passing by I marvelled that they would dare come forth,
I drew my sword to slash them, but put it up again.
Alas alack, the sixth song, its purpose long denied…

Commentators have been baffled in the search for meanings for this and suggest the sequence is an allegory. But again by analogy we might suggest the way a great poet in another tradition uses snatches of songs, ballads and even children's rhymes, putting together chains of association. Shakespeare in *King Lear*, for example, in the stream-of-consciousness ramblings of the Fool in the storm scene, throws in popular song, ballads, children's jingles, Merlin's prophecies and even real-life texts of exorcisms, along with tales of giants, all to portray a mind under unbearable stress:

He that has and a little tiny wit –
With hey, ho, the wind and the rain …
Pillicock sat on Pillicock-hill
Halloo, halloo, loo, loo!

And then a rhyme still recited by English children today:

Child Rowland to the dark tower came,
His word was still, – Fie, foh, and fum,
I smell the blood of a British man.

Is Du Fu doing something similar? Great artists at the top of their game of course experiment with themes and motifs from a wide variety of sources, but this sounds like something more visceral. It suggests the product of a distressed mind, someone trying to hold on to reality in a time of crushing anxiety for him and his family. The repetitions perhaps help him process what is happening to him. Take the lines about the hoe in the second verse:

My long hoe, hoe, hoe, handle of white wood –
I trust my life to you – you must save me now!

When you have nothing left to lean on, falling back on the repetitions of folk song is perhaps a way of trying to cope with trauma.

All in all, the 'Seven Songs' is one of Du Fu's most strange and daring song sequences, and interestingly there is some indication that oral versions of these songs survived on the spot, though precisely how that came about is hard to imagine. Writing over a century later in 873, the local prefect may be talking about these songs when he recalled that 'the Chestnut Station poems of Du Fu are very much remembered orally by men in these parts; but of 120 years ago, is there any written record now?'

Since the eleventh century some Chinese critics have given the 'Seven Songs' very high praise as one of his most important works: 'a poem rarely found in a thousand years,' wrote the poet Zhu Dongren. The eighteenth-century critic Shen Decai commented that Du Fu 'didn't just copy the shape and form of existing poetry but achieved a magical transformation'. But it was an experiment he never tried again.

Perhaps in the end, then, the key to the 'Seven Songs' is not so much technical as emotional. The family's situation was dire. Du Fu foraged in the snow for medicinal herbs and acorns. On one occasion he says the ground lay under such a thick covering of snow that he came back with nothing to eat, and that evening could only listen to his children's groans as they huddled together. It was perhaps the nearest they came to starving to death. His naively imagined Land of Plenty was an illusion. There was nothing for it but to move on again. Further to the south, beyond the mountains in Chengdu, he had friends, especially the local prefect and fellow poet Pei Di, whom he had known years before. So, late that freezing January, on the first day of the first lunar month, when wealthy people were preparing for the New Year with plenty on their tables, the desperate family wrapped up as best they could and set off for the south, the land of Shu: Sichuan.

In the Song dynasty, scholars used clues from Du Fu's poems to piece together this part of his journey. For example, Zhu Mu (an imperial geographer from the Southern Song period) located Du Fu's Bark Ridge at today's Fujia Town, 20 li (7 miles) east of Tonggu. Here local tradition said the family lived by the riverbank, and today there's a modern Du Fu memorial hall for tourists, close by on a hill with wide views.

But the war still pursued him. Though the government held the region round the capital, local rebels now occupied the whole area around Qinzhou, and with raiding parties striking south, Du Fu had to push on. This would have been a forbidding journey on foot in the eighth century. They climbed Mupi Ridge, crossed the valley of Luo at the White Sand ferry, their cart abandoned now, their old horse carrying their luggage, its neighs echoed by the wails of monkeys in the cliffs. They made a night crossing at the Shuihui Ferry Crossing upstream on the Jialing River and entered Sichuan. Coming from the north, the mountains become less of a barrier here – the continuous cliffs break in the middle, where a narrow pass

at the foot is guarded by the 'Sword Gate', Jianmen, the entrance to the land of Shu.

From there the mountains give way to the plains. After the struggles of the previous weeks, numbed with cold and worn out, the footsore and starving family came along the banks of the Jialing River all the way down into the plain of Chengdu. They had escaped.

The plain of Chengdu: for Du Fu, a brief time of peace.

12
Chengdu
'Oh for a huge roof to shelter all the world's poor'

Chengdu's once beautiful plain, the 'Land of Heaven', still has its untouched corners, fringed by the wooded mountains. These woods are dotted with gorgeous shrines, like the magnificent E Mei temple on a mountain range which Du Fu seems to have explored, presumably on horseback, during his time here ('these days I've got to know the old man of E Mei: he knows that idleness is my true nature!'). Here, nestled in forests of ancient pines, is one of the four sacred mountains of Buddhism. At Leshan, an astounding giant Buddha is enthroned in a towering red alcove cut into a tree-clad cliff looking out over the Min River: impassive, giant hands on knees, emanating an immemorial, almost geologic, spirituality. First cut into the red sandstone cliff during Du Fu's youth, it was unfinished in the early 760s when he came here.

After weeks of travel through a harsh and wintry land of peaks and gorges, the family arrived in the welcoming plain of Chengdu. Seventy by thirty miles, the plain is fed by four rivers. Today it's mostly developed, but then it was open countryside, the prefectural city walls circled by a filigree of streams. It is extraordinarily fertile soil, from ancient times a 'land of abundance' with three harvests a year, and there was hardly an uncultivated inch with an astonishing range of vegetables, grains and fruits. The variety of rice strains alone was proverbial, as the visitor can still find in the city's markets and restaurants today.

Most important, Du Fu had friends here, especially the local prefect and poet Pei Di who offered him support. After the war-torn north, you can feel Du Fu's relief to be down

Chengdu today with the Xiling mountains beyond.

south and away from the fighting in his poems from the time. 'Suddenly I'm under a new corner of the sky', he wrote, 'among the mulberries and elms the sun shines on my traveller's clothes. The city is bustling, full of new people ... the splendid houses, the trees – it's a beautiful place'.

The old city of Chengdu has been destroyed by developers since the 1950s. Only a couple of streets are left; a confected traditional China. But it's a pleasant city to hang out in nonetheless. Here Du Fu and his family ate well for the first time in weeks. For today's traveller this is where you will get the first real taste of Sichuan cuisine: delicious street food, spicy tofu and noodles with cold rice wine and lemon juice. My hotel is in a district aimed at the serious Du Fu tourist. The room has calligraphy and landscapes on the wall; in the foyer behind the reception desk is a framed portrait of the poet seated on a rock, wrapped in a gown, with a wispy beard and hollow cheeks drawn by austerity; his head up, lifting his eyes on a distant horizon; a man who could look beyond present sufferings to his future destiny. Of course, we have no idea what he really looked like, but for centuries this is how the Chinese have imagined him. He is a big draw here, and in the hotel district near his house and garden you can find plenty of modern memorabilia.

The Tang Dynasty Leshan Buddha, visited by Du Fu on his way to the Yangtze.

Along with Lu Xun's house at Shaoxing, it is one of the biggest literary tourist pilgrimage shrines in China, visited by old and young, searching for some enduring key to what Chinese civilization has stood for over so long. As one tourist said to me: 'We ask ourselves, what is our relation to this past? Is there still a connection? What is "this culture of ours", as Confucius called it?'

Here in spring 760, given a small plot of land by an old friend, Du Fu built a thatched hut in a tiny hamlet by an old Tang monastery, along the river to the west of the city. The view was magnificent, as Florence Ayscough rendered it literally: 'snow range at edge of Heaven, white.'

Today the cottage is inside urban Chengdu, but mercifully the site covers such a big area that you can easily get lost within its walls and forget you're inside a big city. It lies just beyond the edge of the old city, outside the inner ring road, circled by the Huanhua brook and surrounded by 80 acres of gardens and trees. It's still a gorgeous setting: with its ornamental streams and gardens, huge thickets of bamboo, peach and plum trees, and yellow splashes of wintersweet and jasmine. Old pine trees tower over the walls. Perhaps China's most famous literary monument, the thatched hut itself has been reconstructed with a kitchen at one end: simple furniture, beds and a desk with inkstone and brushes, the tools of the trade. The one real item from history is a millstone which was excavated nearby onsite. Grinding corn on a quern and ink stick on his ink stone: the two daily rituals that sustained him.

The site has been visited and commemorated since before the end of the Tang. The poet Yong Tao (789-873) wrote a poem about the cottage still standing in his day at Flower Washing Creek: 'I recall when the Master was in Shu [Sichuan]: the old residence should remain through the ages' (i.e., as a way of remembering the poetry). In 902 Wei Zhuang found the residence fallen apart and overgrown and 'ordered the thatched cottage to be rebuilt with the idea of recalling the person, not daring to expand its basic layout'. It was the beginning of the Du Fu tourist business in Chengdu. 'You can forget about the sites of his birth and death,' wrote one. 'The Thatched Cottage is the place you have to see!'

But was it on this spot? Some western scholars and commentators have suggested that the whole site is an invention, a fictional recreation like so many in China today, and that we don't really know where he lived in Chengdu. But, in 2001, while laying a drain inside the tourist site, builders found a Tang dynasty site. An archaeological exploration began, and the big excavation has been left and roofed with a railing around the exposed pit. In it you can see the foundations of religious buildings, secular buildings and houses, as well as ceramics and a Tang stele. And this is all actually inside the area of the thatched cottage tourist site. So, it was indeed a

Tang village. The most fascinating display shows the remains uncovered in the excavation: the find of a small Buddhist monastery, with houses, brick platforms and an inscription on a tablet from 687 referring to 'the small tower of the senior monk' (in one poem Du Fu refers to 'the stream flowing in front of the tower of monk Huang'). This has all confirmed in astounding detail the eighth-century tradition tenaciously passed down over more than 1,200 years. Though destroyed and rebuilt many times, this was indeed the very spot; it is here we get closest to him. It is said this is the oldest, if not the most visited, literary pilgrimage place in the world. And here his poetry takes on a new tone:

Here outside the city there are few worldly affairs …
Beside us there is a clear stream to dispel a stranger's grief.
Clouds of dragonflies hover, rising and falling
A pair of ducks dive and swim together …
I have chosen a place to grow old in
Far from the capital I have become a farmer …
The curve of the clear river flows around the village
On a long summer day everything has a secret beauty.
The swallows in the roof come and go as they please …
My wife makes a chessboard by painting paper;
My boys make fishhooks by bending needles.
A man who is often sick needs medicine/herbs:
What else should an ordinary person seek?
Aside from this I want for nothing else.

The approach to the cottage is down a long lane lined with stone walls painted deep vermilion, over which tower huge thickets of waving bamboo. Wandering around the gardens you meet enthusiasts from all over China, smiling visitors braving the wet autumn weather. I bumped into people from Shandong in the north-east, from Guangzhou and from Nanjing. Three

The site of Du Fu's Thatched Cottage at Chengdu.

women came over, as jolly as holidaymakers in Blackpool:

'We are sisters. We come from Yibin City in Sichuan, about 300 km away. We are all over sixty-five – well past retirement age in China. She's the oldest – she's seventy. After we retired, we decided to get out, go on trips and have fun; so here we are!'

'Do you have favourite poems?' I asked.

'There are so many. One we particularly like is "Song of My Cottage Un-Roofed by Gales", which we were reading this morning over breakfast.'

The oldest sister jumped in with a quote:

> *The gang of boys from the village – they think I'm old and helpless, and steal the thatch right before my eyes. I shout at them till I'm hoarse and dry in the mouth, but what's the use?*

'You can imagine him shouting at the naughty children. It's funny; he could laugh at himself, you know – he's not always serious. We came here especially for this verse and got up early to be here when it opened to miss the crowds. Our generation

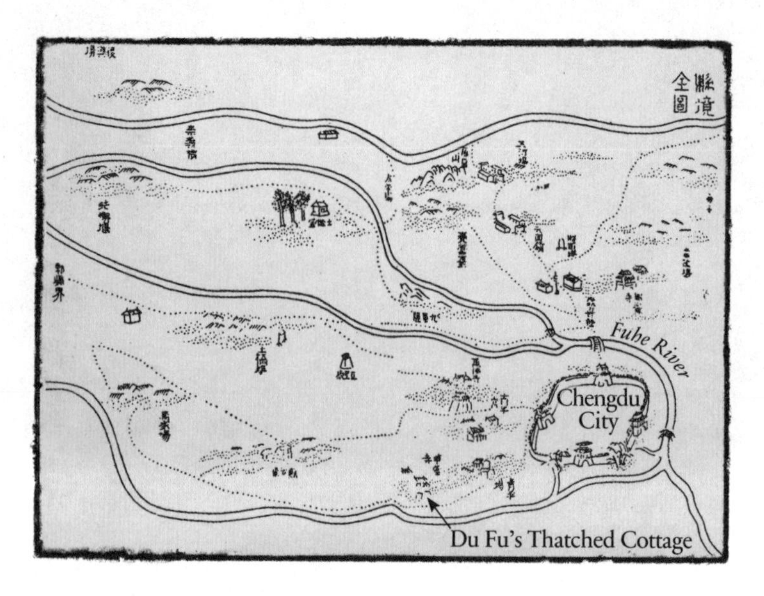

Local gazetteer for Chengdu, 1686, marking Du Fu's Thatched Cottage.

is still very proud that we have such a poet in the tradition. We think his poems are beautiful and still worth passing down to the younger generation. A deep cultural atmosphere was handed down by the ancestors, and his collection of poems is still worthy of our inheritance.' She smiled. 'Though of course we were born in the early years of the People's Republic under Mao Zedong. Life was hard then when we were kids, and we didn't have the possessions and the freedoms we have now. Today is a different generation. Now is a different time.'

Another group of women join us. They are old schoolmates now living in different corners of China from Guangzhou to Hunan and Shanxi, and they have come to stay with their friend who lives here in Chengdu. Clad in bright-red rain macs and matching hats, undeterred by the squalls, they ask for a selfie together. They talk about Du Fu's empathy and the beauty of his words, his 'sincerity', a word that crops up again:

'The poems are really beautiful, and he cared very deeply for the nation. We admire his strength of character in adversity and his sincerity. He has a soul of compassion.'

Outside the hut, a young Chinese woman in fashionable clothes with a digital camera pulled Du Fu into the age of the internet in impeccable English:

'I think in recent years Du Fu has taken on a new life with the internet. There are many websites now which analyse his words and translate his poems into modern Mandarin. His language is difficult – some of it very difficult – and we Chinese all read him today in modernized versions. There is so much junk on the internet, mindless distraction, social media, Weibo, you know; there has been a huge draining away of the spiritual part of our lives, and people are searching for something more. Younger people are latching on to why he's so great. He really is timeless. You travel abroad and look at these websites and, well, you feel proud to be Chinese.' She laughed as if slightly embarrassed. 'In fact, when I'm abroad I read some of his poems, like the ones here at Chengdu, and it makes me feel homesick!'

A young middle-class couple had come with their six-year-old daughter, who was sitting on an inscribed stone reading a Du Fu poem.

'When I was young,' the mum said, 'I was influenced by the ancient poets. We've been big readers since we were young. You see, we were born in China, and traditional Chinese culture has been our big influence since childhood. I always loved reading the ancient poetry when I was a child. We had a teacher at school who loved it and taught us to recite the poems out loud and appreciate the words and also their sound, their cadence. Now I have a daughter and I want her to be influenced by the ancient culture. I really enjoy passing it on to her, teaching her the rhythm of the poetry as well as the feelings of the ancient poets. The first time she heard a poem she loved it and wanted to know more, so I decided to bring her here to see his cottage. It's my gift to her that she can carry with her all her life. That's what led us to come here on a special family trip to Chengdu and the Thatched Cottage.'

The poem her little daughter first heard was the exquisite 'Welcome Rain, Spring Night', which was written here in Chengdu – 'Brocade City'. As the drizzle came and went, I asked her to read it out loud.

The good rain knows its season.
When spring arrives it brings life
It follows the wind secretly into the night
And moistens all things softly, soundlessly.
On the country road the clouds are all black
On a riverboat a single fire bright
At dawn you see this place now red and wet:
The flowers are heavy in Brocade City

It was raining harder now. I took shelter under the trees as a flurry of drops pattered on the leaves. Then an old gentleman came over, diffidently, and said hello in slow and careful English. He was from Chengdu and came to the garden 'at least once a month' to reflect on Du Fu's poetry. For him it was a form of meditation.

'I live alone now; my children are in other places. Du Fu is important to me because he wrote so many poems that express the feelings of the ordinary people. He knew how the common people felt, especially the poor. In one of his poems, he describes how the autumn storm blew away the roof of his cottage, and he and his family were left cold and homeless. He said if only it were possible to build a huge mansion with millions of rooms, to shelter every poor person in the world, everyone would be happy even in a rainstorm, for the house would be as unshakeable as a mountain. "Oh, if I could see such a house before my eyes," Du Fu says, "even if mine was smashed and I froze to death, I would die happy".

'For thoughts like this, Du Fu is in the hearts of all Chinese people. For a long time, we suffered, now we are better off, but today society is very materialistic, and spiritual things are going away. But I feel these things still matter, and here in this place you can go right into his mind: the thoughts and feelings of someone from so long ago. To me, that is a miracle. The garden here is big enough to get lost in, away from the public, especially if you come early in the morning. I sit in a corner and recall him, maybe read one of his poems out loud, and reflect on it.'

He paused, trying hard to find the right words in English: 'Reading his poetry is like meditation,' he said, highlighting a profound difference in the way the Chinese read poetry. In a language with no tenses, no gender, no definite or indefinite articles, the interpretative part of reading, interrogating the roots of the signs, filling in the spaces between signs, is paramount. In China, reading poetry is indeed a form of meditation.

As the skies cleared, I wandered down by the river. For Du Fu, his time here gave him a period of peace while war continued to rage to the north. As the kids grew up, perhaps he even thought he might make it his home. The military governor Yan Wu made him his special adviser, for which Du Fu received an official title and the identity tally of an official, the *yü tai* – the silver fish emblem hung in a red silk bag from his belt, bearing his name. But then, like blood pulsing in his head, the disasters returned to haunt him. There were Tibetan invasions from the west, and rebel attacks from the north. Du Fu realized there was no escape: the war would follow him. The breakdown of the state induced frequent bouts of depression. Chinese civilization idealized moral order, and Du Fu was above all an idealist:

I recall the past, this era's days of splendour…
In the palace the sage ruler, soothed by sacred music,
Throughout the empire, comrades forever faithful and true.
A hundred years and more, no calamities, no upheavals…
But fields sown in grain now flow with blood.

For the European visitor it seems legitimate to see modern western parallels with Du Fu's grief in the poetry of this period, with the sense that the old world was gone and a new one was waiting to be born. Think of Auden in his New York bar on 1 September 1939, seeing 'waves of anger and fear … over the darkened lands of the earth':

The Enlightenment driven away,
The habit-forming pain,
Mismanagement and grief:
We must suffer them all again.
And the lie of Authority
Whose buildings grope the sky:
There is no such thing as the State.

The most poignant comparisons perhaps are the First World War poets. Apollinaire, for example, in that far-off summer of 1914 in his extraordinary poem 'The Little Car':

We said goodbye to a whole epoch
Furious giants were looming over Europe …
We understood that the little car had brought us into a
New age
And that though we were both already fully grown men
We had nevertheless just been born.

Later in the First World War, when all could see that Europe had descended into horror, Sigmund Freud published his *On Mourning and Melancholia*. Overcome by the scale and savagery of the catastrophe, Freud saw that one may mourn as deeply for an ideal civilization as for a loved one. The poetic vision was the same; from Britain Wilfred Owen, Edward Thomas and Rupert Brooke; in France, Charles Péguy, the Austrian Georg Trakl or the Germans August Stramm and Ernst Stadler (who was at Oxford before the war and loved England, where he is remembered in a monument in Magdalen Chapel). All died.

It is no coincidence that at this moment in Europe we see a new engagement with Tang poetry, not as the sentimental poeticizing anthologies of the late nineteenth century, but as a powerful reflection of the contemporary world. Ezra Pound's *Cathay* was published in April 1915 based on the notes of Ernest Fenollosa about Li Bai's frontier poems. Later that year the sculptor Henri Gaudier-Brzeska spoke to Pound of its inspiration. 'I keep the book in my pocket,' he wrote from the Marne. 'Indeed I use the poems to put courage in my fellows. I speak now of the bowmen and the north gate ['Lament of the Frontier Guard'] which are so appropriate to our situation ... the poems depict our situation in a wonderful way.' As Pound had hoped, it was the first intimation of the power and universality of the Chinese verse, an elegiac war poetry nobody until then had written anywhere. Li Bai's 'Exiles Lament', Pound thought was 'like an Elegant Tipperary'; and one hundred years on *Cathay* is still among the most important literary responses to the First World War.

Pound's versions have often been criticized (he knew no Chinese), but the response to his versions of Li Bai's poetry about the An Lushan war was the beginning of real western engagement with Tang poetry. At this point, Du Fu was still little known, but after the horrors of the Second World War he came into his own, not least with his fundamental belief that the artist should bear witness to his times; his war poetry in particular being seen for its universality, transcending the particular time and place to become part of a grand vision of 'human life on earth'.

13

To the Great River

'At the edge of the world'

The plain of Chengdu was a fine place to live, with its emerald-green paddies and golden fields stretching to white-capped mountains. Even today it is still one of the nicer Chinese cities. But just as Du Fu had feared, the war spread south, and then the Tibetan kingdom (a powerful empire in the eighth century) launched a massive invasion into western China and captured Chengdu. He lost his patron Pei Di and again found himself impoverished. For a period of nearly two years from 762 to 764, Du Fu and his family abandoned the Chengdu house and lived north-east of the city in the hills above Zizhou (Santai County), where today a modern 'Du Fu thatched house' stands by the bridge over the Fu Jiang River. For a while he stayed at the Crane Forest Buddhist temple on Ox Head Mountain, likening himself to someone 'going this way and that, snared in undergrowth which was seldom cut

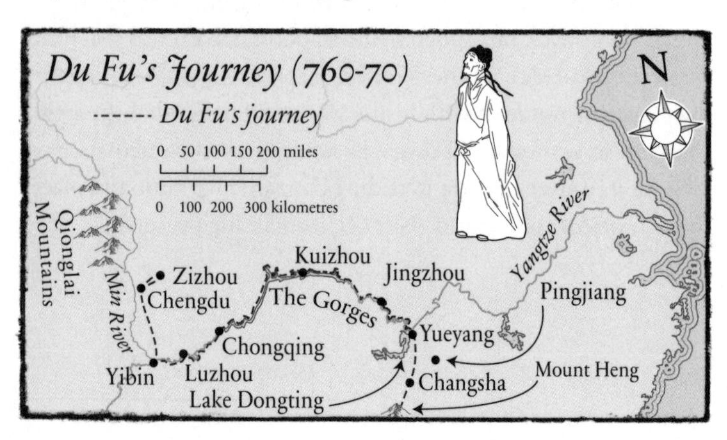

away'. Long walks on the forest paths brought regretful, Zen-touched thoughts:

I should give up being an old man who sings crazy songs
Aim instead for a mind of no attachment

To the abbot Wen, splendidly serene in his isolation (he had never left the monastery in ten years), he addressed a rueful and incisive poem:

For long now I've been tainted by poetry and wine...
I long to hear of that Prime Principle
To begin the first stage of mind cultivation.
With your golden scalpel cut the film from my eyes –
It will be worth more to me than a hundred gems.
With the law of no-birth drawing me upward
Perhaps with your help to reach that Truth

Was Du Fu really so conflicted? If we believe in his honesty, then yes – despite the fact that he was a husband and father of young children. Renunciation was not an option. Though he writes that he was 'longing to begin the first stage of mind cultivation', in fact he was already very well-read in Zen texts. The image of the skilled physician using a golden scalpel to cut the film of ignorance from the eyes of the patient comes from the famous *Nirvana Sutra*. 'No birth' of course refers to the ultimate reality of all things, which as the *Heart Sutra* states, is characterized by 'no birth, no cessation, no impurity, no purity'. But within the longing expressed by the poem, in that place of momentary illusory perfection in Abbot Wen's place of beauty and tranquillity, was the realization that Du Fu was 'tainted by poetry and wine', and however much he longed for Buddhist nirvana, he was too far gone in both. His job, his being, his destiny, was as a poet. And although he tells us there were times when he had to give up wine because of his bad health, drinking went with it.

In 764, as the immediate threat of war receded, Du Fu returned to Chengdu. The governor Yan Wu gave him a job as a military adviser, a token job on a stipend. Yan Wu was an old friend with whom Du Fu seems to have had a close but at times difficult relationship; one time Du Fu was accused of being arrogant and impolite to him, the poet not wearing his cap out of respect for a senior official, and there's a strange story of a furious confrontation, rudely haranguing Yan Wu while drunk at the foot of his bed. Being Du Fu evidently was never easy.

With government victories in battles with the rebels in the previous year in the Central Plains, he began to formulate a plan to get back home by heading down to the Yangtze and then sailing eastwards. On his return to the house in Chengdu, he went down to the river to find his old boat moored there during his absence:

All my life a heart set on rivers and lakes,
Long ago got my little boat ready,
Not meaning it just for clear streams here …
All the time longing for the old hills.
My boat – gunwales I'll never thump again –
Sunk in water a whole autumn by now.
Looking up I see birds winging west,
Look down, shamed by the river's eastward flow.
Possibly I could raise it
Or easily enough find a new one?
What pains me is having to run away so often.
Even a simple hut I can't stay in for long!

In the event he hired – or was gifted – a bigger boat, to take all the family and what belongings they still had. Perhaps he had heard news that war was coming and had decided to escape south down the Min River to Yibin (Suifu). Here, 200 miles from Chengdu, the Min meets the Great River and from here

River commerce in 1902 – still the teeming life Du Fu saw.

in the old days you could get a larger type of travelling barge or riverboat. In his head now the hope no longer of preferment but just to get back to the old family homestead near Luoyang. As spring 764 passed, he again wondered: 'what year will I ever go home?'

Chongqing today: the biggest city in the world.

Following his path, I travelled straight from Chengdu by train, heading south-east across the wide green expanse of the plain to pick up his route again at Chongqing, the junction of the Jialing River and the Yangtze. The capital of the western allies' war against Japan, then against the communists in the late 1940s, Chongqing today is a giant. Its setting is extraordinarily dramatic and the bus journey into town from the north railway station, winding round steep gorges, crossing and recrossing the two rivers, is simply jaw-dropping. The core of the city stands on a sandstone peninsula between the rivers that twist round in steep ravines. In Du Fu's day it was the great inland port for river traffic; on the river you would have seen thousands of boats. To imagine what it might have looked like, this is Florence Ayscough describing Chongqing at the end of the First World War:

> A great junction of water-courses where ten thousand junks assemble, ready to carry the hides, leather, furs, bristles, musk, rhubarb, and other medicines, silk yarn, silk fabrics, insect wax, hemp, iron, copper, and salt – in a word, the riches of Szechwan – down through the Three Chasms to the seaboard at Great River Mouth.

How close to us in time, just a hundred years ago, yet her words are closer to his world, as are early photographs which still show the vast river traffic, when thousands of junks passed up and down Upper Yangtze every year, boats up to 120 feet long with huge oblong sails, the biggest crewed by fifty or even a hundred men. So close in time, but we are so far away now. Now serried rows of skyscrapers teeter up the hillsides, new bridges are thrown up apace as the city expands, the myriad ferries that used to criss-cross the rivers largely gone.

Chongqing is now on some reckonings the biggest city on earth – it looks like it, too. I walk the evening streets head in the sky, breathing in the pure exhilaration of modern China. My hotel is in the centre under a forest of skyscrapers which light up the night. The sheer energy is astounding; it is a place of urban growth like no other on earth. There is no city like it. The next day I took a bus down to the port and the 'amazing copper-coloured waterway which cuts China in half'. Here you get the ferry to continue the journey, eastwards to Baidicheng – and the Yangtze Gorges.

14

Into the Gorges: White Emperor City

'The autumn river kills one with longing'

By now Du Fu had a boat big enough to transport the family and a small crew as far as Baidicheng. Paintings of river boats from the Song dynasty suggest that it would have looked very much like the houseboats which you can still see on the Yangtze today. There was a covered bow where the family bedded down; during daytime the cook worked in the midships with a clay stove; at night the stern was covered with bamboo or rattan screens where the crew slept. It had a single mast with long oars, spare mast and huge coils of bamboo ropes. This would be his home as he sailed down to the Gorges.

Coming down from Chongqing, you enter the first gorge at Wushan, twenty miles long, lined by huge cliffs often a thousand feet in height. It's an incredibly dramatic landscape, as many early travellers recorded. 'Witch's Mountain Gorge is uncanny with the black gloom of a winter day, clouds swirling round the higher summits, and the long yells with which the boatmen besought the river god for a wind,' wrote the Victorian traveller Isabella Bird. At Wing Box Gorge the river narrows to 150 yards wide between vertical cliffs with swirling rapids before it emerges at Kuizhou. There have been big changes of course, but the early photographs help us imagine Kuizhou, 'a large city with a very fine wall and noble gate-towers and imposing roofs of yamens and temples are seen above the battlements.' In the old days, before the Three Gorges Dam, the water rose more than 150 feet in the seasonal inundations after the snow melt on

Yangtze river boat, 1897: the kind used by Du Fu's family.

the Tibetan plateau. Old photos show the landing stages at Baidi recalling descriptions by Song travellers, with a huge jumble of masts, and up the banks a seasonal village of shops stalls, wine bars, repair huts, supply warehouses and tea shops below the city walls, along with smoking brine pits, charcoal burning, and a ceaseless train of water carriers trudging up and down between town and river. All that cannot have changed that much until our time.

The Three Gorges Dam has changed the ancient topography for ever – and the old ways of river life that persisted to the twentieth century. But haunting photographs from a century or more ago show us something of the world Du Fu knew. Described by early travellers, the view east was always delightful, changing hour to hour with distant snow peaks burnished red long after the Gorges had passed into evening. As Isabella Bird wrote, 'the picturesque city, the magnificent opening of the Feng Xiang, the Wind Box Gorge, the hill slopes in the vividness of their spring greens and yellows, the river and its rapids ever changing in texture, was a picture of which one could never weary'. And it seems Du Fu never did. On a creative roll, he wrote hundreds of poems as if transfixed by the landscape and the vast spectacle that unfolded anew every day. 'There are so many fine things here for fashioning my spirit,' he wrote, as he entered a new phase of his life as a poet, in what we might call the artist's journey into the interior.

In Du Fu's day the town of Baidicheng was famous as 'White Emperor City', named after the ill-fated Gongsun Shu who died in AD 36. It is also connected in legend with the 'peerless hero' Zhuge Liang, as Du Fu called him, whose giant bronze statue, cloak billowing, greets the modern visitor crossing the bridge to the island. Today what remains here after the construction of the Three Gorges Dam is a forested island topped by the Baidi temple. The water now is more than 500 feet higher than the low season in the old days so the town Du Fu knew has been permanently flooded, save for the upper part of the hill and the wooded peak with the old shrine now joined to the shore by a long footbridge.

The countryside in the hills was full of small farmhouses growing crops of wheat and barley, root crops with 'juicy leafage, good country paths bordered with yellow fumitory, or earth smoke ... a farming paradise', as a nineteenth-century traveller remarked; and so it evidently was a thousand years earlier.

Landing stage under the walls at Baidicheng, 1897.

With help again from local friends, Du Fu bought some land and at one stage had two farmsteads. His main house was situated away from the town, a brisk hour's walk uphill; his vegetable garden with an orchard and orange grove of almost six acres commanded wonderful views which with a little imagination we can still see in the mind's eye. Sometimes he walked higher up above the Gorges to see the whole vista unfold with distant mountain ranges beyond. So, although the river has covered the site of Du Fu's houses, if we look up, something of the 'landscape remains', as he would say. We may think of him as at times an impractical dreamer and idealist, but his courage, tenacity and resourcefulness on his painful journeys suggest otherwise. Like any Chinese gentleman he was a practical man, often planting, sowing and cultivating his cottage garden. And in time in the Gorges, though he had a little disposable cash, the main source of food for himself and his family was what he

Qutang Gorge below Baidi, photograph by John Thomson, 1872.

planted with his trusty hoe and harvested and cooked. He could smile about it, as in this poem titled 'Planting Lettuce', which he introduces with this note:

> It is autumn now, the rains have come, and I made a small plot by the main house. There I planted a few beds of lettuce in separate rows. It has been almost twenty days, but the lettuce has not yet germinated and only the wild amaranthus is flourishing. An honest man who laments the times may even late in life make a small profit; but it's tough going and I'm making no progress. So, I composed this poem:

Yin and Yang were topsy-turvy,
Domineering, recalcitrant, no longer keeping good order,
Dryness and drought were in their midst…
The good grain crops were almost done for
Then clouds and thunder suddenly took over…
I could make a garden plot by the hall,
I called to my boy to start it out facing me.
Ah lettuce! Common among vegetables
We planted its seeds as you should.
But after twenty days they did not come up,
Buried in mud, and I watched helpless
And you wild amaranthus, you are everywhere
I don't know where you came from,
Spreading over everything
The whole yard is ruined

And inevitably a moral lesson:

Thus I understand how the bad overwhelms the good
Choking it until it perishes
When a garden falls into mugwort and artemisia
Then an old gardener will always feel sad.

The old photographs help us imagine the shift in Du Fu's poetry that takes place in the Gorges. The images taken by John Thomson, who came up here in the 1870s with his developing gear and glass plates, and by Donald Mennie in the 1920s, show the Gorges that Du Fu saw. They capture the life of the river he could see below him from his house: the washerwomen, the woodcutters, the native boatmen and the 'trackers' hauling boats on long cables on precipitous rock-cut paths round the rapids, their straining chests almost touching the stony shores and screes. At the mouth of the Gorges was the city with its walls and gates, its narrow stone-flagged alleys, and the low-season temporary shanty town that grew up below the city walls when the water level rose and fell in its gigantic annual cycle, like a living being. Not surprising, then, that so many Tang poets wrote about it, and that in Du Fu's poetry the river becomes a vast, almost sentient presence, regulating all human existence within its reach, transmitting the pulse of life on earth to the stars and of the stars to earth and the ever-changing surface of the river.

Down here Du Fu found himself outside his own civilization, for the indigenous Chu or Man people spoke a different language and their customs were strange to him. It was clear now that his dream of being the emperor's minister and having his picture hung in the 'Unicorn Hall' would never be fulfilled. 'Long wanderings will be my fate now', he wrote. But as another famous exile, Dante, would say: 'Our Fate cannot be taken from us, it is a gift'. In a sense, then, his exilic situation, despite his frequent bouts of depression, cut Du Fu free. In the Gorges, though it had been at great cost to himself, Du Fu's gift was creative and imaginative freedom.

His poems written here constitute an all-encompassing vision of existence. As the old *Prefecture Gazetteer* noted proudly: 'Du Fu wrote over four hundred poems here. Each blade of grass, each tree, each thing became his theme.' Every aspect of life is a subject for poetry – as Rilke said, a true poet should not only experience cities and people, 'but get to know animals and the flight of birds, and the movements that tiny flowers make when they open in the morning'. Du Fu here is also the poet of the small, the close-up: making a fence, planting lettuce or squash, cooking a meal, playing with his children, meeting old friends, getting drunk – the simple joys of life. One gorgeous poem ends with him on his hillside high above the river coming face to face at dawn with an inquisitive deer at the garden gate:

At my bramble gate – I face a deer; so close here we touch our own kind in each other

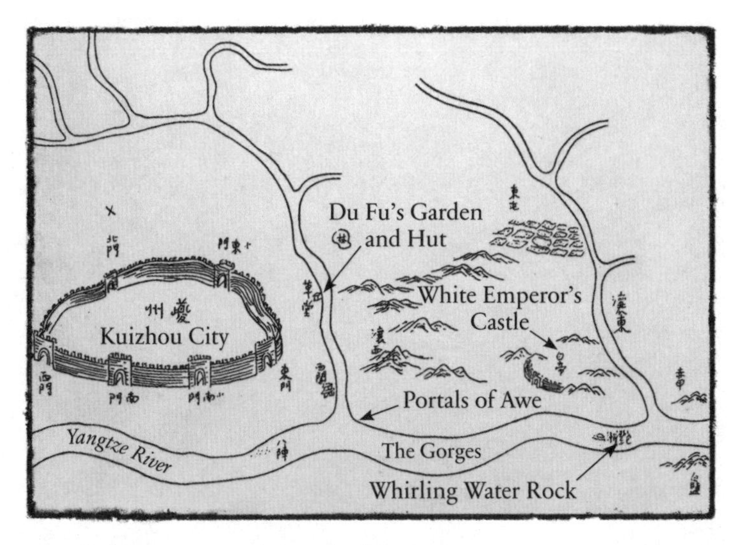

1891 Kuizhou gazetteer: the mouth of the Gorges.

That is – the poet is surely saying – recognizing our common kinship in each other, our common life-being?

Through this time, he also wrote affectionately about his domestic life with his wife and children, wistfully reflecting on Pony Boy's fourteenth birthday:

Young boy, when did we first see you?
On this day deep in autumn you were born…

So far now from the courtly world he had once coveted, he broke all the rules of poetry, for example writing about his servants, calling them by name, and praising them for their efforts, which would have been unheard of in earlier Chinese poetry. He even dedicated poems to them. Suffering from

Following pages: Baidi in 1922: Du Fu's cottage was up to the left beyond the pagoda.

diabetes, Du Fu was always thirsty, and one evening during a local dispute about water, his supply was cut off. His serving boy Aduan went off up into the woods, braving wild animals, found a new water source and worked until midnight to set up a supply to the house through bamboo pipes. In his poem to Aduan, Du Fu saluted his 'rare spirit … amazed that you passed through packs of leopards and tigers!'

It was a creative period in which his translator David Hinton sees him as taking on a kind of 'geologic perspective'. Drawn closer now to the Zen of his teachers, Du Fu had come to terms with the limits of human action in the face of the immensity of nature and time, and his poems from the Gorges have inspired Chinese poets ever since.

But he was always scraping to make ends meet, and hustling for some kind of employment. After a few months, the local governor helped him out with a token job, which gave him a modicum of financial security. With it came accommodation in an apartment in a tower on the city wall in Baidi with a spectacular view overlooking the entrance to the Gorges (see John Thomson's photo on page 110). It was quite a long walk back up to the cottage, especially if drunk on wine, and sometimes – if, say, he had a concert or poetry gathering in town – he would stay there. But sleep was a problem for him now. Back in Chengdu he had remarked: 'since the troubles landed on me I don't sleep much'. Now many poems refer to the periods of the night, signalled by the drum on the ramparts: the midnight watch, or the fifth watch before dawn. In one poem he speaks of being 'half abandoned to sleep, watching the lampwicks curling down.' Sometimes he falls asleep drunk then wakes in the early hours, thoughts flickering – the Proustian memory of the taste of Sichuan spicy mince, or, as in a dream, 'that boat drifting through falling snow'. He complains about his lungs – his asthma now had worsened – and he started to sleep propped up on a high pillow. With diabetes and bouts of malaria, it was hard to ever get a good rest.

Everything was becoming an effort. He had become a habitual night walker, and his poems often describe the night ending and red hint of dawn; awake for the first light on the eastern horizon before radiance fills the sky. In the Gorges poems there is a recurring image of the emptiness of a cold, clear night, 'wide-open at the edge of heaven'. It was a setting and a time to contemplate the story of human life, whether of a single individual, or of human history, set against the immensity of the cosmos. Faced with this vast spectacle, the foundational stories, the great tales of human culture, dissolve and all one is left with is the human mind and emptiness – the absolute clarity of Zen meditation. Human feelings and memories are set against these immense vistas in which the Yangtze (as in Chinese myth) is an extension of the 'great star river' of the Milky Way, the vast circulatory system of the cosmos, in which human lives are integrated into a vision of all nature. The following wonderful poem was written, as the title says, during a 'Night in the Tower'.

In the evening of the year Yin and Yang
hurry the shortening daylight.
On the sky's edge frost and snow
clear in the cold of night.
Drums and horns of the fifth watch,
Give notes both strong and sad,
In the Three Gorges, the river of stars,
reflections stirring, shaking.
Weeping in the wilderness, how many families
know of war and loss?
The people's songs rise from fishermen and woodcutters -
Tales of 'Sleeping Dragon' and 'Leaping Horse'
The old heroes who have turned to dust.
All word of events in the human world lost in these vast silent spaces.

That's Stephen Owen's translation. The multiple meanings of the last line in particular have taxed Chinese readers as well as western translators. David Hawkes reads literally and more prosaically: 'Idle to feel melancholy at the vexations of life and the lack of news from friends and kinsmen'. Burton Watson is more abrupt in his approach: 'Human affairs, word from others – I live utterly cut off from these'. David Hinton attempts a more allusive rendering: 'and the story of our lives just opens away – vacant, silent'.

Night over the Gorges was clearly a time he found entrancing, 'the River of Heaven white from eternity, the Yangtze's shallows limpid from just now'. He sees shooting stars, and the reflection of the starry night in the river 'like pearls from a snapped string', lifted from reality in the stillness of the night; hypersensitive to the faintest sound – a rattling leaf blown by the breeze, a grasshopper shifting its perch. This poem, 'Night', is a lyric that we can imagine Du Fu singing to his guzheng, a plucked zither. This version is by David Hinton:

Crescent moon stilled in the clear night
Half abandoned to sleep, lamp wicks blossom
In echoing mountains unsettled deer stir
Falling leaves startle locusts
Suddenly I remember east of the river (the taste of) mince
And that boat drifting through falling snow.
Tribal songs rise invading rifling the stars.
I am empty aware at heaven's edge

But lest we think him too cerebral, standing outside himself, one poem about returning late to his cottage presents a side of the poet that is easy to forget.

Past midnight evading tigers on the road I return
Home in mountain darkness. Family asleep inside,
I watch the Northern Dipper drift low to the river,
And Venus lofting high in empty space, radiant.

Holding a candle in the courtyard I call for two torches
A gibbon in the gorge, startled, shrieks once.
Old and tired, my hair white, I dance and sing out:
Goosefoot cane, no sleep, Catch me if you can!

David Hinton renders the last half line wittily – skittishly even. The exact sense is 'in this moment who can rival me?'. That is, for all my decrepitude, I would trade my place now with no one, being spontaneously and truly happy. We picture the old man dancing round the dark courtyard in torchlight. In that moment, for all he has suffered, singing for joy.

Following pages: 'Fishermen's songs rise over the Gorges' – photo by Donald Mennie, 1922.

15

Autumn Wastes

'The law of this floating life'

Other great sequences written in the Gorges worry away at these profound themes, changing perspective from the observed outer world to the subjective inner world of personal experience. Most famous in China are the *Autumn Wastes* poems and the eight stanzas of *Autumn Meditations*. These cycles of poems are of fabulous intricacy and almost unearthly chains of word-thought associations. The opening stanza of *Autumn Wastes*, beginning with the same image of the Gorges, the river of stars Du Fu could see from his room in the tower, but this time from the allotment in front of his house, expands over five verses into a regretful but accepting kind of autobiography.

Before we read it, a few notes are in order, just as they would be for a Chinese reader looking at, say, the mythological allusions in a Shakespeare sonnet. The Well Rope Star in the opening verse is the star that presides over the eastern Sichuan region where Du Fu was living. The old man's offering to the fish refers to a Buddhist teaching from the *Flower Garland Sutra.* 'Music and rites' in the third verse are the underpinning of the Confucian way, and 'mountains and woods' are the traditional place of Daoist introspection. In the fourth verse, the Dark Maid is the goddess who sends down frost and snow. The Southern Palace is a constellation, but also recalls a real palace at the capital, where the Unicorn Hall was decorated with portraits of eleven great ministers who had served the state with distinction. The final two lines refer to the story of an official serving in the Gorges region who put a foreign word into his verse at a poetry competition, excusing himself on the ground that he had 'lived too long among the barbarians'. The reader will see too how the sounds of the Gorges vividly imprinted themselves on his mind. Here's the whole of the *Autumn Wastes* sequence in Arthur Graham's translation:

1

The autumn wastes are each day wilder:
Cold in the river the blue sky stirs.
I have tied my boat to the Well Rope Star of barbarians,
Sited my house in a village of Ch'u.
Though the dates are ripe let others cut them down,
I'll hoe for myself where the mallows run to seed.
From the old man's dinner on my plate
I'll scatter my alms to the fish in the brook.

2

Easy to sense the trend in the drift of life,
Hard to compel one creature out of its course.
In the deepest water is the fish's utmost joy
In the leafiest wood the bird will find its home.
Age and decline are content to be poor and sick,
Praise and blame belong to youth and glory.
Though the autumn wind blows on my staff and pillow
I shall not weary of the North Mountain's ferns.

3

Music and rites to conquer my failings,
Mountain and woods to prolong my zest.
On my twitching head the silk cap slants,
I sun my back in the shine of bamboo books,
Pick up the pine cones dropped by the wind,
Split open the hive when the sky is cold,
By scattered tiny red and blue (flowers)
I halt my pattened feet to smell the faint perfume.

4

The autumn sands are white on the far shore,
The glow of evening reddens the mountain range.
Submerged scales push startled ripples,
Returning wings veer with the high wind.
The pounding of washing blocks echoes from house to house,
Woodcutters' voices sing the same tune.
The frost flies down in the care of the Dark Maid,
But the blanket she gives parts me from the Southern Palace.

5

My ambition, to be pictured in the Unicorn Hall:
But my years decline where the ducks and herons troop.
On the great river, autumn is soon in spate,
in the empty gorge the night is full of noises.
The by-paths hide in a thousand piling stones:
The sail has come to a stop, one streak of cloud.
My children too have learned a barbarous tongue,
Though it's not so sure they will rise to high command

When hearing the poem spoken aloud in Chinese, a powerful element is the musicality of the verse, and in this connection, it is worth noting that – as we shall see – oral traditions of the singing of these poems are still handed down in a number of places across China.

In these verses modern scholars have seen the beginning of a change in Du Fu's poetry, and in Chinese poetry as a whole. Arthur Graham suggested that in some cultures a moment comes where language expands to express new ideas, and the nature of poetry changes, becoming richer and more complex; expressing multiple meanings, irony and self-reflexivity. This change took place in English poetry during the sixteenth century, in French in the nineteenth century. Graham proposed that in China, it happened in the eighth century, and is first seen in

Du Fu's work, in particular in his Gorges poems, which influenced the whole of the poetic tradition in China.

These poems were written late in Du Fu's life, and perhaps we might compare them with the late phases of poets in the western tradition such as Ibsen, Yeats and Rilke, and especially Shakespeare. In his late plays Shakespeare took the English language as far as it was possible to go before the modernists; breaking syntax and coining neologisms to a point when one wonders whether he might have begun to lose his audience. Broadening the comparison beyond poetry, one might even mention the last works of some great composers, Bach in his unfinished *Art of Fugue,* or Beethoven in his Late Quartets, which some contemporaries thought 'indecipherable'. Isolated by his deafness, Beethoven perhaps is the classic case of an artist who had reached total mastery of his medium going into deliberate heroic intransigence. May we see Du Fu in the same light? A late phase not of resolution and serenity but stubbornness and difficulty? For all their differences there are common factors in their lives: isolation, ageing, the exilic sensibility; but it could not be said that Du Fu ever rejected the literary community to which he belonged. A great artist at the peak of his powers, in his 'late style' he continued to challenge his readers, as Stephen Owen says, 'taking the Chinese language as far as it could go ... and no one later took it further'.

This is particularly so with *Autumn Meditations*, the poetic sequence from Kuizhou which many Chinese readers consider, along with *Autumn Wastes*, to be the greatest words in Chinese poetry. The eight verses tell the story from the beginning of a day in Kuizhou, with the first stanza being the preface and each one afterwards forming a chapter. The description of Kuizhou and the Gorges narrates a twenty-four-hour period through morning to morning before widening out beyond the stars on the horizon. The last verse seems to be a dreamlike

memory of a courtly outing in the countryside near the capital, but by jumbling word order and disintegrating syntax, he creates a poetic form so experimental, daring and bizarre that it anticipates the Imagists of the twentieth century (who themselves drew inspiration from Tang poetry). In Chinese, as we saw in his early poem about Mount Taishan, this device is known as inversion, the inverted word order called *dao zhuang* in Chinese. It is not an uncommon trick in Tang poetry as a way to make the sentence more lively and surprising, but Du Fu – who had spent his entire life thinking about poetry and had complete command of metre and sound – took it further.

Autumn Meditations is a world in itself; its eight eight-line stanzas framed on the 64 hexagrams of the I Ching. The opening two lines refer to landmarks in the region of the capital, then the next four lines are almost a dream reflection, like shards of memory recalling an outing in the area of the capital. It is literally impossible to translate, and in the last couplet Du Fu himself seems to be saying something about the limits of writing itself. The whole eight-poem sequence ends with a magical memory of the past fading, coming back to the point of Du Fu's writing brush, perhaps defeated in the attempt to capture the fleeting moment. Indebted to Burton Watson, a literal version might resemble something like this:

Kunwu countryside, Yusu river, a twisty winding way
Purple Tower Peak, shadow falls into Meipi Lake.
Fragrant rice, peck, drop, parrots, grains,
emerald parasol tree, nest, grown old, phoenix, branches.
Gathering kingfisher feathers with lovely ladies, we talk together in the spring,
(or gathering spring gifts of kingfisher feathers?)
with immortals in the same boat, set out again in the evening.
Once my many-coloured writing brush stirred the very elements;
now I mumble, gaze into the distance, white head bitterly bowed.

'Women as fair as goddesses' – the world of the court.

Trying to make grammatical sense of lines three and four in English might yield:

> *Parrots peck, dropping grains of fragrant rice;*
> *On the branches of the emerald parasol tree the phoenix grows old*

With the poems written in the Gorges what is unsaid is crucial. On this aspect of his poetry, there's a perceptive note by the critic Wei Tai, the disreputable younger friend of the reformer Wang Anshi, who was writing at the close of the eleventh century. Garrulous and funny, and a great fan of Du Fu, Wei was interested in the subliminal way poetry works on the mind of the reader or listener. In his 'Eight Poems on Grief', thinking of Du Fu, he says this, an observation pertinent to all poetry in any language:

> Poetry presents the thing in order to convey the feeling. It should be precise about the thing and reticent about the feeling, for as soon as the mind responds and connects with the thing the feeling shows in the words; this is how poetry enters deeply into us. If the poet presents directly feelings which overwhelm him, and keeps nothing back to linger as an aftertaste, he stirs us superficially; he cannot start the hands and feet involuntarily waving and tapping in time, far less strengthen morality and refine culture, set heaven and earth in motion, and call up the spirits!

16

The Dancer

'Fifty years passed like the turning of a palm'

One night in late autumn 767, just before Du Fu left the Gorges for good, here in Baidicheng came the chance meeting we described at the beginning of the story. A guest in the local prefect's house, he saw a dance performance by Lady Li, who – as Du Fu discovered when he spoke with her afterwards – was a pupil of the great court dancer Gongsun, whom he had seen perform when he was a child. He recorded the precise time and place, as if it was especially important to him, crystalizing his feelings about the power and beauty of art, and its transmission over time. Gongsun, 'with her crimson lips and pearl encrusted sleeves', was long gone, but in her later years she had found 'a pupil to whom she could transmit the fragrance of her art', which Li had conveyed

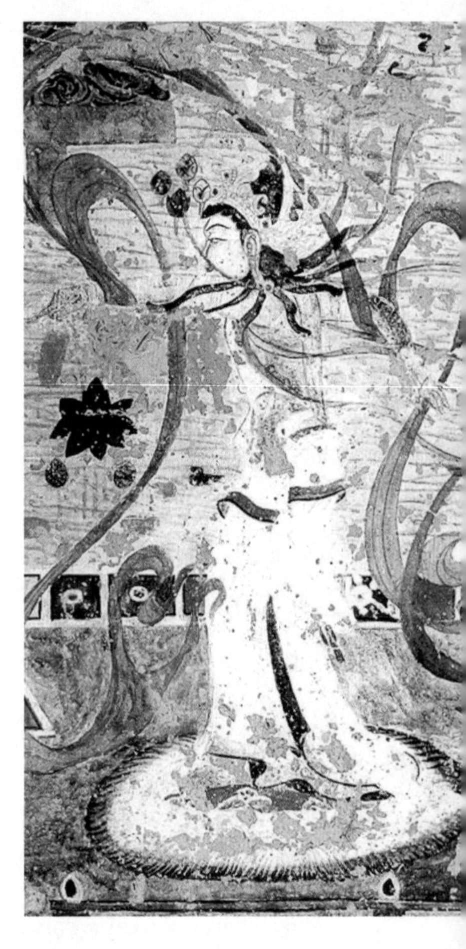

'Like a deity on a flying dragon' – a Tang dancer.

'with superb spirit'. For Du Fu, this thought aroused complex and painful emotions, which he recorded in a twenty-two-line introduction explaining the circumstances around the composition of the poem:

> On November 15, 767, at the house of the vice-prefect I saw the Lady Li from Linying perform the sword dance. Marvelling at her agility, I asked who her teacher was. 'I'm a pupil of Gongsun,' she said. And I remembered that day when I was still a child, when I saw Lady Gongsun herself perform the sword dance ... And where now is that lovely figure in her gorgeous costume? Now even I am an old white-haired man, and her pupil is well past her prime. But having discovered her pupil's history *I now realized that what I had been watching was a faithful reproduction of the great dancer's interpretation*. The train of reflections set off by this discovery so moved me that I felt inspired to compose a ballad about it.

After his magnificent description of the dance (see page 23), the poem ends with this reflection:

Since then fifty years have passed so fast, like the turning of a palm.
Stormy waves of war have enfolded our royal house in gloom.
The pupils of the Peach Garden have scattered like disappearing mist;
and here is this dancer with the cold winter sun shining on her
fading features.
The brilliant feasts, the music and the song have ended ...
After pleasure, comes extreme sorrow
The moon rises in the east.
And now I depart, an old man who does not know where he is going ...
Feet calloused from wanderings in wild mountains
Ever more weary of this hurrying world.

17

Downriver to Lake Dongting

'A sand gull blown between earth and heaven'

Early in 768 Du Fu and his family moved on once more, and from now on fate begins to close in on him. There has been much debate about why he left Kuizhou. It has been speculated that he had heard news that the war had rolled away from the Luoyang area and that now, after long wanderings, he thought he might be able to sail downriver and then head overland to his old family home.

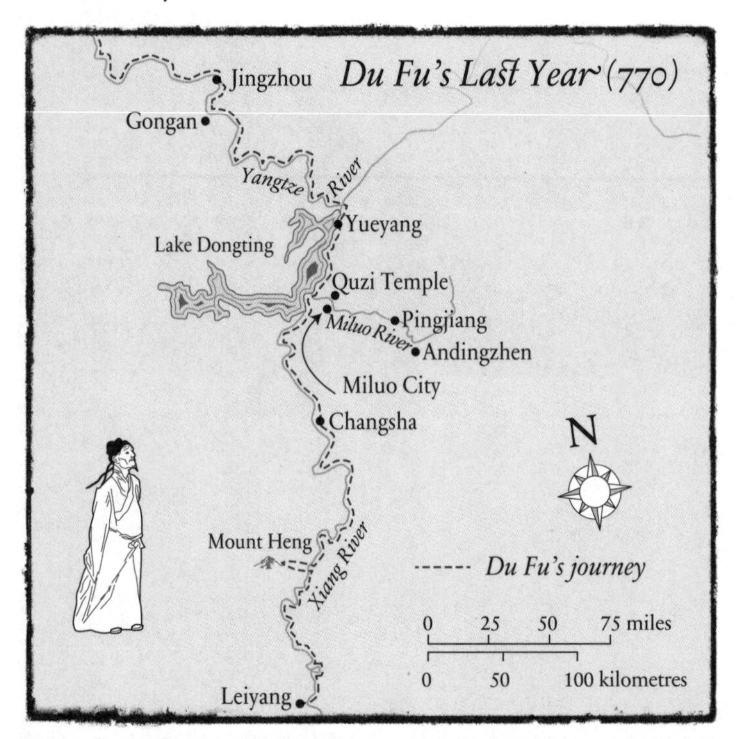

In late autumn, his newly married younger brother Du Guan arrived in Jingzhou and seems to have sent letters telling Du Fu to join him, perhaps offering some kind of support. At any rate, after more than two years in Kuizhou, Du Fu decided to put his affairs in order and leave. He entrusted his fruit orchard to a local family and gave his cottage to a kinsman with instructions to help a poor lady next door with whom he had shared some of his garden produce. The woman was destitute, with no surviving sons, and he had allowed her to take fruit from his garden. Please don't build a fence between the two gardens, he wrote – that would not be kind.

She told me the officials have bled her dry
When I consider what the war has done to us all, it makes me weep.

Before he left, his friends held a parting banquet with wine and musicians to see him off. Then he and his wife and children trooped down to the landing stage where the boat crew waited. So in the second or third week of February, Du Fu and his family set off eastwards through the Gorges. In an atmospheric poem, he describes the flood of sadness he felt as they boarded the boat that would take them to their new home:

But getting on the boat I find myself unhappy.
When the mooring was untied, I alone gave a long sigh . . .
Turning into the narrows, apes howl in the depths.

Today you can follow their journey by river, though now the track is broken by the Three Gorges Dam. From Baidicheng, I signed up for twenty-four hours on a tourist ferry. That night the basin was lined with big Yangtze cruise ships: giant gin palaces with lights blazing from stem to stern. With forty or fifty jolly Chinese tourists I took a smaller, more old-fashioned boat: rather like a traditional Greek ferry, with a purser's desk, thick red carpet in the foyer, brass Art Deco-style doors and a

Jingzhou: Du Fu and his family stayed here through the summer of 768.

curving marble staircase. Below deck the crew's clothes hung on washing lines in the gangways. I confess, it was my kind of boat. There was a mah-jong house, bridge room and a circular polished wooden dance floor on the upper deck – sadly unused these days.

The cabins are basic, but fine; they serve hot water, but – and it's a first for me in China – no tea. Luckily, from years of habit on the road, I always take an emergency supply of teabags just in case. I stayed up for a while hugging the old brass rail, hoping to glimpse the Starry River in its splendour, but all through the night clouds obscured the heavens; Du Fu's Well Rope Star was nowhere to be seen. And so, through the night we sailed eastwards down the three great Gorges through which over millennia the Great River has cut its path to the sea – aided, as Chinese myth has it, by King Yu the Great, the primordial controller of the waters, with his helpers Yellow Dragon and Black Turtle.

The journey through the Gorges is nearly 200 miles; a leisurely week's sail for Du Fu, but he was delayed with bad weather. There was an accident at the rapids where Du Fu's boat, 'bobbing in the waves amid whirling eddies', was driven onto rocks. 'My books and histories were ruined, our baggage half crushed and soaked'. This necessitated a stop to repair and dry out. 'All my life,' he wrote ruefully, 'I have teetered on the edge of disaster; but in this moment I escaped the place of my death, and broke out finally into a flat river.'

Our ferry thankfully avoids the rocks and stops at the port before the dam. Then it's a bus to Yichang, where the sky clears after days of autumn cloud over the Gorges, to reveal blue hills fringing the horizon to the east. Tramp steamers and barges run through the night; it's a nice place to hang out on the journey downriver. On the main street there are good restaurants specializing in the 'dry and spicy' Hubei and Hunan cuisine: hot pots, smoked meats and fermented beans – back on the menu as autumn draws in after the summer months of damp, subtropical warmth.

From Yichang I followed the short distance east to Jingzhou. It was a desultory day when I got there, grey and rainy, spindly chimney stacks over the rooftops, the river now a mile wide. The city lies on a big curve of the north bank of the Yangtze with a fine, partly wooded river frontage, and impressive weathered Ming walls and towers in places topped with vegetation.

The family stayed in Jingzhou for several months from March 768. After the incredible productivity of Du Fu's time in Kuizhou, only about twenty poems survive from here, most of them verses for social occasions when the composition of a poem was expected, or when he was trying to butter up a local official and get patronage. His frequent talk of parties suggests that he was drinking heavily again after a period in which he had given up alcohol. Was the creative urge ebbing in him?

Was he perhaps not inspired by the landscape in the way he was in the Gorges? Was he ill? Or just gloomy? (Some poems have titles like, 'Getting Rid of the Blues' and 'Driving Out Depression'). The climate was enervating; through that summer he complained about his worsening health and the stifling weather.

The 1877 local gazetteer points out the place where Du Fu stayed, a down-at-heel lane in Shashi district just behind the waterfront, now overlooked by drab blocks of flats. The street sign still calls it Du Gong Xiang, 'Du Fu Alley'. The northern end is a narrow stone-flagged alleyway till recently lined with pretty wooden balconied courtyard houses from the late Qing dynasty, which are now sadly mainly bricked up. Down the lane there's a whitewashed temple gateway with terracotta tiled roof and blocked windows, the sign over the door reading Qing Long Guan, 'Green Dragon Temple'.

Here locals say was the 'Little White Pond' Du Fu wrote about (several old fishponds survive in this part of the city, although the one close to Du Fu's home is long since filled in). The poem they say was written here is 'Little Whites' or 'Minnows' (whitebait was a Jingzhou speciality). It is about what we would call sustainable fishing; about not eating the eggs of any species, bird or beast, whose adults are hunted or fished for food:

Little whites: each in the school is given a life.
A fish by nature just two inches long.
Thin and tiny they stick with their watery tribe.
By local custom, they go with garden vegetables.
In the market a tangle of silver flowers
poured from a box – insubstantial flakes of snow –
their lives when we collect their eggs,
what right is there in taking them all?

A metaphor for rapaciousness that has no thought for the future? Du Fu has similar poems about the needless killing

The southern entrance to Du Fu Alley before demolition in the 1990s.

of other creatures – deer, birds, and even insects: 'when the world in in disorder', he wrote, 'the lives of all living things become unimportant':

Those who wear robes and caps of office are also brigands, rebels;
They love money, they love food, and snatch them in a twinkling.

As for Du Fu Alley, the south end was demolished more than thirty years ago and the little white pond is long since filled in. Green Dragon temple is boarded up and due for demolition. But a preservation order has been placed on the northern end of the alley, as a site of cultural and historical importance, so all is not quite lost. A last glimpse.

It was not a happy time. Despite his brother's welcoming letters, hopes of support evaporated. Had Guan been called away? He had no cash, no local gentlemen officials who might help him out, and he was reduced to doing menial jobs. After the tranquillity of their time in the Gorges, he seems to have split up for a while with his family, lodging elsewhere. He soon came to regret making the move from the Gorges. 'I've come to this land for nothing; I regret parting from like-minded friends.' In the somnolent heat of high summer, he abandoned the alley and slept on his boat moored outside the city wall. 'I should just study to become a river god,' he observed drily.

In my twilight years, the bitterness of being swept along
This evening, weeping from war and separation.
My children often write urgent letters,
Not even having gruel with goosefoot for dinner,
How did it all come to this?

Looking back over his adult life, he'd spent fourteen years on the road, driven from place to place, seeing terrible things, often fearing for his life and most of all for his wife and children. They had faced starvation; his infant son had died of hunger.

It would be incredible were he not suffering from some kind of post-traumatic stress. In his verses he describes a heavy physical toll, and the psychological hurt may account for what he admits was a frequent need to cry:

Drink before me, I face my guest and let myself weep:
Do you not sense that this old man feels a wounded spirit within?

At Jingzhou, all the old anxieties had returned, and he was back on the drink. At one point he says he had 'almost given up on poetry, only my medicine chest matters now'. Ever the great sightseer, he still made trips into the countryside on horseback, but nowhere was safe, with bandits and armed gangs on the roads. In the autumn he seems to have reunited with his family and they moved on once more, downriver to Gongan. There, governor Wang was kind to him; on one occasion Du Fu recalls sending someone to help him back to his lodgings 'when I was completely drunk'. He stayed at Gongan till winter – 'a village on the sands, covered with snow still frozen with ice'. But, inured to rootlessness now, 'so long a wayfarer', he found himself disparaged by strangers, his kinsmen offering no long-term support. Things were closing in. Late 768, he left downriver by small stages to Lake Dongting, still carrying in his red-silk pouch his badge of office, the battered silver fish bearing his name.

I followed him on the last major leg of his life's journey by train. The true pilgrim with time to spare would have followed his route all the way by boat, down to the junction with the Xiang River, before turning south into Lake Dongting. But my time was limited and so I went across the plain by train into Hunan. The landscape opens out now: a vast irrigated green plain, mile upon mile of paddies, lotus farms, vegetable patches, fields lined with poplar trees, and villages strung out on long country roads. Everywhere now in the countryside, as prosperity

Yueyang Tower on the shore of Lake Dongting.

grows, people are constructing two- or three-storey buildings, and all around them the red soil of Hunan. But to stay precisely on his track one should go down Dongting Lake and make one's way to Changsha by water, sailing by the celebrated Yueyang Tower.

In the rainy season the lake grows to seven or eight times its size. When fed by four major rivers, it becomes an inland sea of freshwater a hundred miles long, a vast shimmering expanse where flocks of migratory birds rise in clouds. It defines provinces (the names Hunan and Hubei literally mean 'north of the lake' and 'south of the lake' respectively). Then ocean-going ships can sail up to Changsha, where, according to local myths, a dragon king lived in underworld fairy grottoes at the bottom of the lake with the wives of the mythical sage king Shun.

Du Fu kept his boat close to the shore of the lake, stopping as he always did when he reached memory places. On the west shore, he tied up the boat and climbed the famous old pagoda called Yueyang Tower. It has long since been rebuilt, but still provides the same view Du Fu saw. His poem about it is shot through with loneliness and despair, though his feeling of gloom would lift when he reached Changsha.

Yueyang Tower

I had heard of the waters of Dongting
And today I climb up Yueyang Tower –
Wu and Chu divide to east and south,
Here is suspended the cosmos day and night.
From friends and family, not a word,
Old and ill, only my solitary boat;
War horses are north of the passes,
I lean on the railing, tears flowing.

18

Changsha

'My road – in the end where will it take me?'

Changsha lies at the southern end of Lake Dongting, a city of ten million people today. Here the rising of 1910 precipitated the fall of the empire; events witnessed by the young student Mao Zedong, whose giant sculpted head with the long flowing hair of a romantic revolutionary and poet, carved out of a rocky outcrop, looks out from the little island opposite the promenade. Old photographs show low-rise city walls and boats. A photograph from 1910 still shows a pre-modern Chinese city with medieval walls running along the river.

Today the old town has been swept away and rebuilt, but there is still an attractive river frontage along the Xiang, the modern high-rises softened by the presence of a vibrant tree-lined corniche, which is crowded with music and dance every morning and evening. The west bank opposite is still uncultivated, with wild horses roaming and straw-hatted

fishermen living in thatched huts, offering glimpses of an older world. On the riverside there is a grandiose memorial hall pavilion to Du Fu on the site outside the north gate, where he is said to have lived (according to William Hung, he anchored at the northern end of town and rented a place by the post station and the fishermen's wharf). Today's huge tourist installation doesn't exactly aid the visitor's imagination, but it is a pleasant and cool place to sit with tea and buy a Du Fu souvenir.

I booked into a small hotel near the riverfront and wandered around the neighbourhood to sample the local night life, sauntering between blocks of flats where old folks sat chatting in the warm evening – men in singlets, lamplit street stalls, busy mah-jong parlours. Further along the street a new tower block housed a nightclub in the basement with thumping drum and bass, a gym on the ground floor, and a restaurant on the first floor named 'Brother Tian Bao' (a nice omen – it's the reign name of Xuanzong, 'the Brilliant Emperor'). The place was heaving; outside people were waiting under an awning, and over the road there was an overflow shed where you placed your order on your smartphones using the QR code on the wall by the fridge.

Changsha: the waterfront of the old walled city in 1902.

The food was traditional Hunanese cooking: lots of chillies, pork, fish and river crabs, and the 'little white fish' which are a staple in this part of the south, as Du Fu had observed. But there was also plenty for a vegetarian like me: wok-fried cabbage, lotus roots, green beans, smoked tofu with rice and an ice-cold Tsingtao beer. Du Fu was a cook and lover of food, and I imagine he would have liked it here: take his poem 'Cold Noodle Soup':

Fresh noodles from the nearby market,
combined with the juice and crushed sophora leaves,
put them in the kettle to do them quickly
I eat quickly, worrying it will soon be gone.
Emerald freshness shines together on the chopsticks,
Fragrant rice along with reed shoots.
Passing my teeth it is colder than snow,
I urge others to eat, offering them like pearls.

I had come to Changsha simply to get to the end of the story, but down here in Hunan the tale opened out in a way I had not foreseen. Earlier in the journey it had emerged that Du Fu and other Tang poets not only came down to us through printed texts but also through oral tradition, through what the great scholar of Islam Louis Massignon called 'living chains of testimony' – families who over a thousand years had passed down the poetry of the mystic Al-Hallaj despite the prohibition on disseminating his work on pain of death. With Du Fu the tradition had been preserved not only in the printed books and teachings of scholars but in village schools, family schoolrooms, poetry clubs and even funeral recitals by traditional 'masters of ceremony'. In these alternative ways poetry in China has been passed down in a self-effacing act of loyalty to the past, even through cataclysms like the communist revolution. And it was down here in Changsha that I found myself touching on these roots of the Chinese poetic tradition.

19

Singing Poetry

'An old man singing crazy songs'

The next day dawned a limpid morning, the sky a wash of eggshell blue across the river to the sandy wasteland where wild horses shake their tails, and old men fish from patched-up tents. Truly the landscape of the south is beautiful, as Du Fu said. I met Professor Yang Yu in the tearoom on the second floor of the Du Fu memorial tower. One of her interests is the living oral tradition of poetry and the possibility of reconstructing the ancient music that might have accompanied it. Research on ancient poetry and music is an expanding subject in China these days. Professor Yu herself comes from Changsha, and currently among their projects she and her students are trying to imagine the music Du Fu would have known, played on instruments which have been reconstructed on the basis of surviving examples of Tang instruments.

'It was a time when popular poems were set to music,' Professor Yang Yu told me. 'Some poems were written to be set to music, so though he was not well known, Du Fu must at times have collaborated with musicians. We want to know how this worked; we have made replicas of Tang instruments to work out how the poems of Du Fu and Wang Wei might have sounded. *Might* – of course, no one can know for sure as no musical texts have survived from this early, even though the instruments have.'

That Du Fu knew musicians is clear. Among his poems is one which probably refers to a concert he attended at an official's residence here in Changsha. 'Meeting Li Guinian South of the River' is about an old musician, Li Guinian, who had been

Changsha today, from the Du Fu pavilion.

famous in the courts of Chang'an and Luoyang when Du Fu was a young man. (As a young man it was said Li had 'the voice of a demon' – a voice that could conjure spirits.) This short poem is one of Du Fu's best known; learned by every Chinese child at school, it is a poem of beautiful economy of expression:

Meeting Li Guinian South of the River

I often saw you in Prince Qi's house
And heard you several times in Lord Cui's hall.
Truly the scenery south of the river is beautiful
And here, in the season of falling blossoms I meet you again.

Du Fu's poem takes us back to the 720s, when he was in his early teens. Again, as with the poem about the dancer Lady Gongsun, references in the poem give us a precise clue. The lords Du Fu mentions, Prince Qi and Lord Cui, died in the early 720s, so he must have first seen the musician play when he himself was around twelve years old. And now, forty-five years later, fate had brought them together again. Prince Qiu and Lord Cui were eminent members of the royal family, figures from the golden days of Emperor Tang Xuanzong. 'And now we meet once more'. Autumn has come, the blossom is falling, the year is dying. The Tang age too? And of course Du Fu himself? The big things are left unsaid, but always present below the surface. To the Chinese reader these unspoken feelings and allusions are all understood.

'It would have been very common for poets and musicians to work together,' says Professor Yu. 'It has probably been the case all along. Poetry sung by famous musicians is the equivalent of today's pop songs. If a musician persuaded a famous poet to write for them it elevated their status, and equally if a struggling poet worked with an established musician, it helped them gain fame too.

'It's possible Du Fu actually worked with Li Guinian. Li Guinian had been Tang Xuanzong's favourite musician, so he frequented high officials' and noble lords' family concerts, like the one in Prince Qi's mansion. I assume that when Du Fu meets Li Guinian again in the south, they met at a Changsha official's concert. Maybe in the governor's house. It's even possible they collaborated, but there's no record of it. Du Fu, by the way, we know could play the *guzheng*, the zither.'

'Do we know how much of Chinese poetry was sung?' I asked.

'So many poets in the Tang dynasty are lyricists. You see, that is to say, Chinese is a tonal language, and Chinese poetry and music are often inseparable. They go together. In fact, though we think of the poetry as the lyrics, the music is there in the tones. It's a pity we don't have any of the original settings.

We don't pretend that the Li Guinian poem as sung by our students today is what it sounded like in the Tang dynasty, because the gap in time is too long. There is no way to precisely recover that feeling, so we are forced to reconstruct. But when we try setting Tang poetry to music today, we do our best to follow the four tones of Chinese characters, to present the style and emotional resonance of Tang poetry.'

The key instrument was the *qin,* the seven-stringed instrument which uses strings of twisted silk. Three or four thousand settings of lyrics for the *qin* (including many Tang poems) survive in printed books from the early Ming onwards. From the Tang only the instruments survive, some perfectly preserved and still playable, such as those in the temple treasury at the Shoso-in shrine in Nara in Japan. (They are the most coveted instruments in the world: a Song dynasty *qin* went recently for $22 million, by far the most expensive instrument ever – putting a Stradivarius into the shade!)

'In the Tang Dynasty', Professor Yu continued, 'these instruments were very popular. For example, take Li Guinian. He was the best singer of that time, and one of his close friends Wang Wei, who was also a very famous poet, was also a musician, especially good at playing the *pipa* [a four-stringed lute very popular during the Tang as a solo or orchestral instrument]. These, and the flute, the *xiao,* have been the Chinese instruments for thousands of years. So, if – or when – Du Fu wrote poems for Li Guinian, he must have written them for the instruments and with the tunes that were popular at that time. But the tradition of oral singing of Tang poetry has lasted for centuries in villages outside Changsha, and in a few other places in China. We've been collecting songs from the countryside where poems by Du Fu and Wang Wei are still sung and have been picked up by musicologists in the last thirty years. Some of these settings possibly go back to the Song dynasty.'

From her handbag she pulled out her smartphone.

'Listen to this. This is a local lady singing the Li Guinian poem.'

It was only about a minute or so long, but so haunting, like a sound from the deep past; a beautiful plainsong whose lingering semitones eerily (to my uneducated ear) recalled the folk music of the far west of Ireland. It was uncanny: a poem I had only ever heard in Chinese in a school classroom in Yanshi recited mechanically by the pupils here took wings. It was deeply affecting in its delicacy, its plaintive quality, its reticence. Chinese friends to whom I have played this since say the singing sounds incredibly familiar to them. 'I think I must have heard similar tunes at funerals or other occasions when I visited grandparents,' said one. So, the tradition was still alive.

Transcription of the singing of the Li Guinian poem, by Armand D'Angour.

20

The Singer of Songs

'The dharma says I am a fool to follow poetry'

Professor Yu put me in touch with her main contact in the Changsha tradition of singing Du Fu's poetry. Cao Qin is about fifty years old, full of boundless energy and enthusiasm. She's a woman on a crusade to preserve and pass on the tradition of poetry singing, which has hung on over the past seventy years, despite the communist revolution and then today's headlong pursuit of materialism. The draining away of the spiritual life and of traditional ways of doing things has been the modern fate of all of the traditional cultures in the world, of course, but is somehow more stark here because the pre-modern civilization of China survived into the twentieth century, only to be deliberately wrecked after 1949.

'Singing poetry among old folks still survives round here and in many places in China,' Cao Qin told me. 'Indeed, you could say it is making a comeback.'

Her teacher and mentor was a man named Shi Peng, who had initiated Cao Qin into the chain. He died in 2019 at the age of ninety-four; I had just missed him. He was from a classic rural small-town Confucian learning: his grandfather passed county level exams and was a teacher in a tiny village school with never more than six or seven pupils. Shi Peng's father had been an expert, as she put it, 'in the *zuo* tradition' – the old literary culture. Shi Peng learned to sing poetry from the earliest age, from around three years old.

'He always used to say that when we do a normal reading of poetry, it feels two-dimensional and flat, but when we apply tunes and expressions (with our chanting or singing), it becomes three-dimensional. And it's the best aid to our memory. Singing has always been the way that poetry was taught, it's a traditional art blended with the beauty of music. It goes as far back as the Spring and Autumn period (around 500 BC). *The Analects* has a reference to Confucius and his pupils chanting 300 poems. Since the imperial examination system was established during the Sui dynasty, the singing of poetry became even more popular. Singing was without doubt the best way to learn poetry or classical texts.'

The story of how Mr Shi built up his vast repertoire is a tale in itself.

'He first learned from his father and grandfather,' Cao Qin continued, 'and then from sitting at the feet of old people in the 1930s when he was a teenager. That was through the time of the Japanese invasion and the civil war. By then he was working for the local highways department, but also did a bit of journalism on cultural topics. That got him into trouble with the anti-rightist campaigns from the late 1950s, and he spent three years in prison; then he was sent to do labour in the countryside.

'Then came the Cultural Revolution, which set out to smash the "Four Olds": old ideas, old culture, old customs and old habits. Du Fu and the poets were all those things. The Red Guards even smashed his tomb in their anger. Shi spent seventeen years working on a collective farm, and his vast memory of oral poetry was his consolation, his sustenance in hard times. Poetry was his life blood.'

As I listened to this story, my thoughts went to Du Fu's own concerns about preserving his poetry and passing it on. Remember his telling remark about Lady Li and Lady Gongsun, that Gongsun's pupil had delivered 'a faithful reproduction of the great dancer's interpretation'? Gongsun had found someone to pass on her art. How tenuous it must at times have seemed. Du Fu carried his own poetry in rolls in a 'book box'. Had his sons not preserved his poems after his death, there was no guarantee that they might not have been destroyed by war, or just thrown out by later generations.

Continuing the story of her teacher Shi Peng, Cao Qin went on: 'After Mao died, China's "Reform and Opening Up" happened from the late 1970s, [and] he was rehabilitated. Then he started a poetry club with like-minded friends. He did it for the pleasure, but also to preserve and pass on stories from the past. They would gather to sing together. In the last ten years of his life, he focused on promoting the ancient poetry singing tradition of the Hunan region.'

When he got older, Shi Peng's friends and colleagues were aware of what he had stored in his memory and wanted to find someone who could pass it on after him – it had to be person to person, there was no other way. So, they looked for 'a trustworthy person of good integrity' and decided Cao Qin was the one. In a formal ceremony at a banquet, she was adopted as his daughter and became his pupil and his heir. This she has done with incredible energy and devotion, carrying on the torch, often running calligraphy and singing classes in the evenings after her day job. She has recorded elderly people singing poetry across Hunan, mainly of the generation born in the 1940s and 50s, but as the word has spread through local literary associations, she is getting younger members now, people in their twenties.

'There was certainly a strong tradition of poetry singing in his part of the country, around Changsha. But other places across China maintain this tradition: Guangzhou in Guangdong province, Hejian in Hebei province, Fuzhou in Fujian province, and Beijing (where it is known as *Guozijian* chanting). Changzhou in Jiangsu is another place, down in the Yangtze delta. This was a very great centre of scholarship, culture and poetry for centuries after the Ming dynasty, and though it was badly wrecked in the

Taiping War, the tradition survived and was passed on. But the strongest atmosphere of poetry singing is here in Hunan.'

Her story seemed to me part of the perennial battle of memory over forgetting. Pre-modern China was still largely an oral memorizing culture, even after the advent of mass publishing in the eleventh and twelfth centuries and the subsequent rich book culture under the Ming and Qing dynasties. Now, though, since the pervasive evolution of the internet and social media, with the best will in the world the traditional memorizing culture is hard to maintain. This is not only the case in China, of course. In my own travels over the years, in South India, for example, I have seen the number

Changsha: the Du Fu pavilion and the Xiang River.

of those with deep conversance with the classical language in Telugu in steep decline. In Tamil Nadu, the memorizing of the vernacular Tevaram poets has been orally transmitted from Du Fu's time, and even before, by a caste of singers called oduvars, but also at home in families, especially among women. It is still strong today; at festival time one may invite oduvars to come to the house for recitals. But the future is not secure. We live in a time where there are so many other pulls on young minds; the time and effort required to master these vast stores of traditional knowledge is daunting.

So, how far back does the singing tradition of Du Fu's poetry go? Du Fu himself, after all, describes teaching youngsters how to sing his poems. After his death there must have been people – and not just his sons and daughters – who knew how to sing his poems, and no doubt passed their knowledge on. His poems were handed down after his lifetime through his manuscripts and copies disseminated from them. For a long while this was not through printing, of course; the earliest datable printed book, *The Diamond Sutra*, comes from 868, a century after Du Fu's death, so the early collections were all handwritten. An early manuscript anthology of Du Fu within ten years of his death contained 290 poems, a mid-ninth-century collection used an authorial original (perhaps through the family), and a larger collection was released in 987. This is testimony to his growing status before the great manuscript edition of 1039 (printed in 1059), which included 1,405 poems, most of his surviving work. The whole chain of transmission then must in the end go back to his own manuscripts and other people's copies which the eleventh-century editors collated.

Oral transmission played its part later, through poetry lovers. This must have been through friends and recipients, but also the *sishu*, the old-style private schools, a very ancient tradition in China. The *sishu* went back as early as the Spring and Autumn period, right down to the Qing dynasty and the Republic, so is over 2,500 years old. These private schools were usually set up by families who had a school room in the house. There was no curriculum, grades or exams; the teacher tailored the teaching to individual students, and would have included favourite poems by well-known poets whose works were passed around and copied in manuscripts. Singing poetry was part of the tradition.

The singing of poems was also preserved by 'masters of ceremony', the hired performers who used to conduct family rituals, feasts and funerals, and which still can be found in China. 'This kind of recital is increasingly out of fashion these days,' Cao Qin told me, 'but you can still see them in the Dragon Boat Festival in Miluo City quite close to Changsha. There, at the Quzi temple, they pay respect to the ancient poet Qu Yuan and hold ceremonies where even now elderly people sing suitable poetry, including Du Fu, and a master of ceremonies will sing the eulogy. That's where you'll still find them.'

21

At the Quzi Temple

'*The* Songs of the South *summon me*'

The Quzi temple lies out in the countryside between Changsha and the lake. The setting is beautiful: green Hunan countryside and red earth. It's near Miluo City, about 50 miles north of Changsha by the Guluo River, at the point where it flows into the Xiang River and Lake Dongting. The town itself stands in a lovely landscape of emerald-green alluvial plain fringed by pyramidal hills. It was here that the first great named poet in Chinese poetry died by suicide. Qu Yuan (*c.*340–278 BC), according to tradition, composed the *Songs of the South*, which along with the *Book of Songs* is the greatest collection of early poetry in Chinese civilization. So, Quzi is a very special place in the story of Chinese poetry.

Entrance to the Quzi temple: literally 'the temple of Master Qu'.

'Old Master Qu', as the locals still call him affectionately, died somewhere near Miluo City where he spent his last years. A loyal councillor and a poet of great gifts, he was unjustly slandered and killed himself by drowning in the lake, tradition says, on the fifth day of the fifth month. The story is widely commemorated today in the annual Dragon Boat Festival. From an early age this was a story that had a special fascination for Du Fu, and he alludes to it several times in his poetry. One might almost say Qu Yuan haunted him. It is certainly uncanny that Du Fu's own personal journey 'of ten thousand miles' over so many years should have led him in the end to Dongting, and the very place where Qu Yuan drowned himself. It was almost meant to be.

'We like to think of the Miluo as the "Poetry River of the World",' said a jolly local visitor. 'Why? Because of Qu Yuan, our earliest ancestor poet – the god of poetry in China. And Du Fu of course, whom we call the "Poet Saint". So, here are the two holy places of the two great poets. We are the people of the Miluo River, and we revere both of them.'

So, you could say the Quzi temple, in a sense, exerts a force field in Chinese poetry, endowed with a kind of poetic and spiritual aura. Smashed and restored many times, wrecked in the Cultural Revolution, the temple today is approached by a flight of steps up Yusi mountain. At the top is a triple gate painted with wide red bands; from the terrace a fine view over the river across to Lake Dongting. First built in the Han dynasty and dedicated to Qu Yuan in the Song, the shrine as it stands was built or refurbished in the 1760s in the reign of Qianlong. In the outer hall, the account of Sima Qian from his *Shi Ji* (our only real account of Qu Yuan's life) is engraved on the wall in gold lettering on black stone. In the inner chamber is an altar room with hanging red lamps, where sacrificial ceremonies are held, especially at the time of the Dragon Boat Festival. Behind the

Commemorating Qu Yuan at the Quzi temple.

altar table is not an image of a deity but a black memorial tablet of the poet with gilded letters. You could hardly find a better illustration of the importance of poetry in Chinese civilization.

Qu Yuan's imaginary portrait hangs in the inner chamber. The authorship of the poems in *Songs of the South* or *Songs of Chu* is disputed, but he is generally credited as their main author – most notably of the extraordinary poem *Li Sao* ('On Encountering Sorrow'), one of the most mysterious poems in Chinese literature. Written at the news of the fall of the capital of Chu to the Qin, *Li Sao* is unlike anything else in Chinese poetry, the great precursor to Du Fu and all the Tang poets.

Slandered by corrupt ministers and sent into exile, Qu Yuan is said to have wandered the countryside collecting the folk songs and poems which were preserved in the *Songs of the South*.

Quzi temple courtyard.

He was later revered in legend as a water god, king of the Water Immortals, in Taiwan, Korea, Vietnam, Singapore and everywhere in the Chinese diaspora. After 1949 he has been built up as the first great patriotic poet, pictured on stamps and latterly celebrated in the Dragon Boat Festival – actually a fertility festival much older than his time but now tied to his tale. Today, he's a model for the loyal, unswervingly moral official who cared for the state.

A small crowd gathers in the temple courtyard as four men prepare for their recital. Old-fashioned country folk, all in their seventies and eighties, they wear formal clothes, Mao suits, three in charcoal grey, one blue, the uniform for the older generation in China during the early days of the PRC. All are retired now; ordinary men, a farmer, a local government officer, a middle school teacher, they are part of a local poetry club, the Miluo Poetry Association; they do it for the pleasure. One of them begins hesitantly, then they grow in power, singing verses solo and then together as a group. They divide the poem in a way that doesn't exist in any printed text, singing the first three characters of each line, then the last five, then the whole line; then they all sing the whole line together again. This way of singing is called *die chang*, which roughly means 'overlay singing'. It is used extensively in 'seeing off' or 'goodbye songs', customary verses prolonging the goodbye with the offer of a final cup. The tradition of singing these poems varies region by region; each area has different ways of dividing the verses.

They start with a famous farewell poem by Du Fu's contemporary Wang Changling, who was killed in the An Lushan war. It's the kind of thing you'll still hear from grandparents or at funerals, saying goodbye in the way that at a wake in Ireland one might sing 'The Parting Glass'. Then they sing a haunting Du Fu poem about music. Like Li Guinian, it has seven characters per line, four lines, again broken up in the four-part descant. It's called 'To Lord Hua'.

In Brocade City the music of pipes and strings is heard all over every day
Half enters the wind on the river, half enters the clouds
This melody should only exist in heaven.
How many times can one get to hear it in this mortal world?

At the end they bow and shuffle as if slightly embarrassed by the emotional power they have created. In that moment it felt as if they had crossed the great barrier of the destructions of the twentieth century and the attempt to erase the memory of China's past, to find that the memory had carried on; not just of texts, but of custom and ritual and ways of performing. It was still alive. For now. For the future, who knows?

22

Du Fu's Last Year

'Thinking what war has done to us'

The last evening in Changsha I met Professor Yu again on the corniche after classes. I was still thinking about the kind of person Du Fu was. As a young man he was privileged, arrogant, typical of his class. It was a time when he thought the world was his oyster, before his failures dented his confidence – not only in himself but in his future too – before he found himself in a stark struggle for survival. From the anthologies today we tend to imagine the older Du Fu, kindly but a bit thin-skinned, melancholy, over-fond of drink, sick, but perhaps also a bit of a hypochondriac. Professor Yu sees someone else:

'I think the young Du Fu was just like all the young people at that time, just like Li Bai: full of passion and hope for the future, and with a special confidence in his own ability. Remember, he was a young man of the Tang dynasty in its heyday, so even though he failed the imperial examinations in that time, he was not discouraged, and felt that he would be able to do it next time. All young people have that kind of confidence and that kind of hope for the future. And when the war began, remember, Du Fu was not that old, and he was still optimistic for the future. Then he was hit by harsh reality. He began to focus on what was happening in the world, on the conditions in which the poor lived their lives. Through that time, Du Fu himself became one of the people. He is no longer the noble son, no longer the young, confident and heroic poet; he has become a common person struggling among countless hardships and tribulations. His depiction of suffering comes from his personal experience, of course, but he always connects his own experience to that of the people and subordinates it to the bigger fate of the times. This is one reason why I think his poetry is still timeless and universal.'

I wondered about his faith in the ideals of civilization. Does he end up stripped of all illusions about human nature?

'I think Du Fu remained an idealist. He always had a firm ideal, which we can generally say is a Confucian ideal of what politics could be. Therefore, his ideal of devotion as he said, "to the Emperor Yao and Shun, and then to the common people", never changed in his whole life, even when his life was turned upside down by the war of An Lushan. This ideal was always central to him, which is one of the reasons he is still so admired by the Chinese people today.'

The poems, I suggested, add up to an intimate portrait of a person, with all his foibles. He lets us see everything. Few people before early modern times tell us more about their daily life, how they thought and felt. When we look at personal memoirs and letters from the western classical age, and the early Middle Ages, rarely if ever do we get so close to someone. Professor Yu paused, pouring the tea as a warm breeze picked up from across the river.

'You know, from when I was very young, I liked Du Fu very much. The reason is not only his sincerity, his expression of the weight and suffering of life. I think many young people especially appreciate that he often also shows a very happy and optimistic side despite the pain, whether in Chengdu, or in Chang'an, or in Changsha. I think the fire of happiness in this pain can move people very much, and then we can feel a kind of unquenchable hope of life, which is always in the foreground. Despite everything, to me that's the key thing.'

Later on, I walked down the corniche in the soft breeze, the last sunlight dappling through the trees. Watching the evening dancers jive and waltz to a live trio with music box, saxophone and guitar, it was easy to imagine Du Fu and other artistic exiles swept by the tides of war, congregating down here – like the south of France in the 1930s or Casablanca in the Second World War. A few months' calm, sunshine, friendship and renewed creativity. But his stay in Changsha ended again in war. In early summer 770 one of the Hunan commanders killed Du Fu's friend Cui Guan and raised a rebellion in Changsha. 'Blazing fires last night', he wrote, 'great columns of smoke singeing the heavens, we were hiding away with fishermen and merchants.' Du Fu fled the city with his family, first to Hengzhou, 100 miles to the south upriver, then further to Chenzhou, where a maternal relative was prefect. A sense of finality:

Fleeing Troubles

In his fifties now, an old man, hair white,
North and south fleeing the troubles of the times…
In the ten thousand leagues of Heaven and Earth
I see no shore with a place for me.
My wife and children also follow me.
I turn my head, joining them in sad sighs.
My home region is a vast wasteland,
Everyone in the neighbourhood has dispersed.
From now on the road back is lost,
I have used up my tears on the banks of the River Xiang.

23

The Last Journey

'Deeply sensing that I have betrayed my life'

For us there's a last journey; fifty miles from the city into the Hunan countryside. It's surprisingly unspoiled, with lush green fields and wooded hills. Finally, after a day or two of rain, we came into good weather, and when I checked into the Pingjiang Sunshine Hotel, its forecourt was drenched in sunlight. The town is on the up; 'a mini Hong Kong', the hotel manager said. For the evening meal the waiter helpfully warned me that Hunan chillies are especially hot. I met up with a London friend's mum and dad; before my trip uncle Yang had done a recce of Du Fu's memorial hall in the countryside and sent photos. They were looking bright and jolly as we posed for pictures outside the hotel door, Yang in a crisp shirt and slacks; Tina's mum in a stylish black trouser suit; even in rural Hunan, China is rising.

Next day is a lovely morning. Just outside town, past the Miluo River, there's a recently restored Tang temple high on a steep hill, reached by a winding dusty track through a forest of broom and mimosa; the bright yellow ochre walls dazzle against a translucent blue sky. Inside, rows of fresh inscriptions on slate grey tablets attached to the temple walls give long lists of new local donors; the new rich of the county anxious to record their charity in the old way, to recover meaning in their lives, still seeking auspiciousness. From the terrace there's a wonderful view over rows of soft wooded hills stretching as far as the horizon over a green bend of the river that flows down to join Lake Dongting. These perhaps were the last landscapes Du Fu saw, though for him the green hills were now covered with frost and snow as a bleak autumn went into winter. This is 'Year Ending':

The year draws to a close with many north winds
The Xiao and Xiang rivers and Dongting lake lie amid white snow
Fishermen's nets frozen in the winters cold…
I hear everywhere sons and daughters are sold,
Kindness is cut off, and love crushed to pay taxes.
On top of every city wall, war bugles are blown.
When will there be an end to such sad music?

The circumstances of Du Fu's death are not entirely clear. He was heading south to Chenzhou but was held up by flooding at Leiyang, where a kindly magistrate Mr Nie had sent him food and drink. Legend said he became ill from eating that food.

'Throw a poem into Miluo river': the Miluo at Pingjiang.

On Lake Dongting: 'nimble gulls swooping over shallows'.

But he didn't die at Leiyang – he turned back towards Changsha and Lake Dongting, the watery world haunted by the spirit of Qu Yuan. So, was he on the main river Xiang or on the smaller stream, the Miluo? After all, he *was* buried near the banks of the Miluo, so if he died at Changsha, why was he buried here? Had he taken the smaller river for safety to avoid armies and brigands and robbers?

His last poem, tradition tells us, was written on the boat in winter 770. It has a few little personal details: the old armrest to steady his now weak hand for holding his calligraphy brush.

His phrase 'excitement gone' refers to a hexagram of the great book of divination the *I Ching*. As for 'wind sickness', in Chinese medicine, wind is 'the spearhead of all disease', most virulent of all the climatic forces that cause disharmony in the human body. It primarily hits the lungs, and Du Fu had long been asthmatic, but now it was more serious. Had he had a stroke?

Here is an edited version of his last poem. His brief prose introduction to the poem goes back to the earliest printed editions and is evidently Du Fu's own explanation of the circumstances in which the poem was composed, just before he died. Even as he was dying he was writing poetry, and his child's death still wounded him:

> Lying on my sickbed in the boat with a 'wind illness', writing my feelings in 36 couplets. Respectfully to be shown to my friends in Hunan

On my journey I am sick and time closes in on me...
This watery land engulfs the simple cottages in a mist,
Maple shores layer green summits...
Excitement gone, now nothing troubles me....
Rushing madly at last where do I go?
Of but meagre talent I take my leave of those I admire;
My black leather armrest is sewn together in many places
My raggedy clothes have been patched every inch...
A dandelion puff tossed along, burdened by cares,
Walking out my medicine, sick and miserable.
In burying a child who died young, I emulated Pan Yue...
I have got to know the customs of all the nine regions of China
And still the blood of battle flows as it has for so long
And the sounds of armies stir to this day...
In taking care of family, and in the secrets of the cinnabar pill
[the elixir of immortality]
I have achieved nothing and my tears fall like rain

His tomb is about ten miles down a country road to Anding, a mile or so south of the Miluo River. On the way we stop for lunch in a cavernous general store and eatery whose proprietor improvises a lunch of spicy rice noodles and vegetables sautéed with chilli peppers. An old boy in the corner suggests a diversion via a famous sacred tree in a valley in the flood plain of the Miluo River, by a rural temple founded for fishermen which has recently been given a makeover with tiled façade and marble floor. Someone makes herbal tea and on the parapet wall a ninety-year-old local with a wide-brimmed straw hat

Memorial hall at the Du Fu tomb near Pingjiang.

and a beaming single-toothed smile regales us with legends of the local gods of the river. It's a place of myth and legend. A dragon king lived at the bottom of lake in an underworld of fairy grottoes with his fairy wives. For us, a last contact with his world.

A little further on, we reach Gaoping village in Anding. The local poetry group, the Tieping Poetry Club ('Iron Vase Poetry Club'), is another channel for memory. Dedicated to passing on the knowledge of traditional poetry, the building was originally a farmers' library dating from Qianlong's day, founded as a public reading library with over 10,000 books. The club itself was originally founded in 1885 – the year is important, as the Sino-French war would end that June in Beijing. Foreign concessions were growing. Down here the literati and supporters were deeply torn; it was a time of profound concern about the culture. Was the old mental universe still meaningful, still of value? Was the traditional culture a hindrance, as many said, 'eating up the children of China', as Lu Xun, who was a child then, put it later? Or was it still itself a means of rejuvenation, as the poet Zheng Zhen had believed? A century or so on, in our age of often gross materialism, those questions are no less meaningful.

So now the poetry society has been refounded in the recently restored ancestral hall in the neighbouring village of Andingzhen, where it coexists with Fashion Home Furnishings and the Chengfa Beauty Salon. There's a lovely wooden hall with outbuildings, framed photos of the restoration round the walls. Outside is a pond where the local kids play. Here enthusiastic locals have formed a reading group to explore Du Fu and other Tang poets. Some of the hundred or so members are local farmers who have a passion for literature. There are people who worked in the city and have retired and returned to the village; there are also primary and secondary school teachers, some retired, some still teaching. For them the 2020s are *just* the time to hold onto the eternals, and Du Fu above all put what they feel into words: the still pre-eminent value of Confucian loyalty, virtue, benevolence and goodness, and the basis of familial, political and spiritual order. For them Du Fu's poetry is a still-living testimony to the continuing greatness and value of their ancient civilization. And the imperative that it is passed on to the next generation, as one of the women told me:

'In our circle here, we often read Du Fu poems aloud together. His spirit has inspired the Chinese people for a thousand years. His poems are full of duty and fond feelings for the motherland. He loves the people and cares about their sufferings. He was a great soul. The more we read him, the more we feel a kind of power handed down across the generations.'

Her friend chipped in: 'He is a very realistic poet. His words have always encouraged Chinese people. We are his offspring. I feel his spirit is still here. In these times this matters.'

Finally, perhaps there is the issue of morality in civilization. For, after all, despite the horrendous violence and cruelty of its history, China was, or aspired to be, above all a moral order. And this ideal was most steadfastly expressed by the poets. But to what extent does that still exist under the Leninist CP of the 2020s? To what extent do the poets still have a role? Indeed, is poetry one of the ways the people try to hold onto 'this culture of ours'?

24

Remembering Du Fu

'Since the beginning of time there was no one like him'

The present tomb and memorial hall is a couple of miles south of the Miluo River, 10 miles south of Pinjiang in Xiaotian village. The site has been rebuilt many times over the years, the last forty years ago to repair the wrecking of the site in the Cultural Revolution. At the time of the restoration, they retrieved Tang architectural remains, including column bases which are now on display. The tradition that the place is linked to Du Fu is a very old one. According to a local historian, Deng Rongsheng, who has researched the family and written on the local dialect, 'based on the set of etiquette back then in the Tang, if the father died, the descendants must stay with the tomb of the deceased and observe mourning customs for three years. Otherwise it's considered a breach of filial piety, almost a crime. So the story goes that Du Fu's sons built a thatched house near his tomb and stayed there. With the local government's help, they even managed to buy some land and expanded their home next to the tomb.

'Their accent had attracted a lot of attention, because they were obviously not local, so people were curious. They knew the family came from the wider outside world, that the dead man had originally been some kind of official from the capital city, so they looked up to them. Later when they discovered that Du Fu was a great poet, they were in awe of them, and hoped that their offspring would look up to the Du family and be learned people who knew the classics and had good manners and civility. This is from the local stories told through generations.

Du Fu's tomb near Pingjiang.

'There are stories of a drought that lasted three years during the Guanghua years at the end of the Tang [about AD 900]. Even the Miluo River had dried up. It was very hard for people and animals. But there's a well less than ten metres from Du Fu's tomb that still provided drinking water throughout this difficult period. The well is very clear, the water quality is superb. It survived flood, drought; you can still always see the clear water. This was considered a good omen. For centuries people from the countryside around have come for water during the dry seasons. According to the ancient customs of Pingjiang, in the old days people had to follow the rules of the heavenly deities. For example, the mountain god, the earth god and the god of the well all have their jurisdictions and territories. So, for people to have to go to faraway places to ask for water, it's considered a plea to their deities. And when you do it at Du Fu's tomb, it's automatically thought you are asking for water from Du Fu himself, as the spirit of the place. So people who came for water all pay respect to him, and kowtow to him, even ask for blessing from "Zimei god", Du Fu's courtesy name.

'According to local tradition there was even a belief that drinking the water made anybody who drank it smarter and promised them a brighter future! The well has remained until this day. Since it was rebuilt in 1884, there's been an endless stream of people visiting, especially when anybody has a child going for an imperial exam, they come here from Changshou Street, Guanyi Ridge, Mufu Mountain, Zhongxian Ping, Jinpu Guan, Xiaotang Pu, Yugong Bridge, all to ask for blessing in the exams.

'Also there are traditional country folk from Liuyang and Changsha, even Tongcheng in Hubei province and Jieshang in Jiangxi, who trek for ten to fifteen days on a kind of pilgrimage to Du Fu's tomb to wish for good fortune in the civil exams. Despite the changes of the last seventy years this still happens; in China things have a habit of lasting!'

It's ironic that Du Fu became a kind of tutelary spirit of the land, despite having failed the exams himself. As for what happened after his death, the best bet is that his sons bought land here and buried their father, hoping one day to return him to the old Du clan family plot near Yanshi. It's a lovely complex. It was restored and expanded in 1883-4, with a hall for the original Pingjiang Poetry Society. There's the memorial hall and tomb, the well, ancillary buildings, and a walled courtyard with a colonnade that's open to the sun where an old tree is hung with a cascade of red ribbons like a sacred tree in a temple. It's a gorgeous scene, with light slanting through wooden screens, radiating contemplative calm – although the walls are daubed with Red Guard slogans from the time of the Cultural Revolution in 1966. Then young radicals broke open the tomb to 'eliminate the remaining poison of feudalism' and daubed the buildings with their dreams for a new future freed from the weight of tradition. They smashed the tomb open, but Du Fu's remains were gone; all that was left was a stone lamp and fragments of rotten silk.

The graffiti of the Red Guards remain on sunlit walls. Scrubbed off but still readable, through them a different past speaks: 'Love People, Country, Science'; 'Share wealth, property, share money'. History still visible like a red scar. Somehow it seems appropriate. No poetic ivory tower, Du Fu's work is muddied and scarred, loaded with the irrational cruelty of war and human suffering. How marvellous that he still speaks to us through all the upheavals of Chinese history, from An Lushan and the Fall of the Tang to the Japanese invasion and the Cultural Revolution. For that reason, the graffiti have been left, for they are not the desecration of history, but history itself.

The last restoration of the tomb was undertaken in 1983 when Deng's 'Reform and Opening Up' not only opened China to the market but began the attempt to recover her destroyed past. In the memorial hall there's a large bronze of the poet, and his biography from the early ninth century carved on black stone on the interior wall. Only forty years after his death, its words were prophetic: 'Since the dawn of poetry there has been no one like him.' It was then perhaps that his remains were moved back to the family graveyard in Yanshi, close to Gongyi, where we started this journey. The cemetery still survives behind the local secondary school; a big tomb with a stone wall and a tall Qing dynasty stele commemorating him: 'Mr Du Public Works Department', the highest civil service rank he attained.

A beautiful day. Blue sky, early light. The end of the journey. It's a very atmospheric spot. Though little visited, somehow it feels more powerful than the monument behind the Yanshi school athletics track where perhaps his remains rest today. Some of the descendants of his sons stayed here in Hunan –

the current Mr Du lives nearby, rheumy-eyed and taciturn, but proud of his ancient ancestor:

'I am a descendant in the fifty-eighth generation – that's what it says in our family tree. Du Fu's son Zongwu, "Pony Boy", guarded the tomb. Forty years later his grandson wanted to take him back to his hometown in Henan. But in the troubled times they couldn't, so they stayed. Today eight hundred people around Pingjiang are descended from him. Of course, I am proud. He is a great poet; he loved his country and he loved the people.'

Now every year on Tomb Sweeping Day, the Qingming Festival, when the Chinese remember the ancestors, the clan hold a ceremony here. The present Mrs Du makes tea and cakes for visitors in her little house in the village, the local schoolchildren file in in school uniform and lay flowers, local dignitaries make patriotic speeches.

China has been through so much in our lifetimes, with the devastation of the Mao era, the Great Leap Forward, the Great Famine, and the Cultural Revolution. But the losses were cultural, too: the wrecking of heritage, the erasure of family records, burned in cartloads in the villages. The aim had been to sever the link with the past, to erase the memory and create new allegiances. But Mao did not succeed. Today every child in China learns Du Fu's words in school: the meeting with the old musician, the spring scene in the ruined capital, the dancer Lady Gongsun, his wife alone in the moonlit window. They are taught about his moral sensibility and love for the common people – and also, of course, his loyalty to the state. In his ambition to save the nation through a career in government, Du Fu was a complete failure, but through his poetry he perhaps did more than any emperor to help shape the nation's values, expressing what it means to be Chinese in the greatest words in the Chinese language.

Epilogue

At the end of my journey I spoke to the diplomat and sinologist Nicolas Chapuis, who is publishing the first complete translation of Du Fu's work in French. It has been a life's task for him, every poem accompanied by notes and commentary. He is optimistic, even bullish, about the value of translation, indeed as many translations as possible:

'I'm convinced more and more', he says, 'in the value of translation. Chinese literature need not remain opaque to the outside world, there are real intersections: the one can illuminate the other and there is no separation between east and west. The gaps are totally arbitrary. You can use Chinese texts to understand western philosophy, and you can use western philosophy to understand Chinese texts. The same goes for the poetry. Du Fu after all was writing about the human condition – what it means to be human. There are differences in approaches and perceptions, but culture is global. Many of the things that China thinks are unique to China are not. It is global; it is human. And it is in poetry that you find human nature. For Chinese poetry has always been about the individual, the personal. And Du Fu above all is the Chinese voice that reaches across the barrier of translation and lives today with a clarity and power that cannot but astonish us.'

Looking back on my own journey in Du Fu's footsteps, his poems in hand, one of the things that stays with me so strongly, even in translation, is the dazzling breadth of this intimate record of the thoughts and feelings of a person of the eighth century. Has anyone earlier than him ever recorded their life in such detail and with such awareness and sympathy? From the tremendous poems about war and human suffering, and the cosmic visions of humanity and nature which he wrote in the Gorges, to the poems on gardening, or building a fence? Fish on a market stall provoke verses about sustainable fishing. Coming face to face with a deer at dawn at his garden gate arouses feelings about our kinship with animals. The loss of his 'kindred tree' blown down by a storm leads to a meditation on its own life force. There's even the tribute to his faithful old horse. Taken all in all, it is an account of the interior life of a man with all his foibles, his joys and sorrows, his punctured *amour propre*, his hypochondria, his love for his wife, children and friends – and his identification with suffering humanity as a whole. When we look into the past, it is the voices of the people of the past that we most hope to hear, and for China, his, above all, is the voice. Are there such things as universal values in history? Du Fu tells us that there are; that for all our differences, at root we humans think and feel the same.

Let's leave the last word to the poet himself. Not long before he died Du Fu wrote a poem about poetry, entitled 'Just a Note'. I'm going to end with this. I have reordered his lines for what I think is better effect in English, but I hope not in a way he would dislike.

Great literature is for a thousand ages.
Whether it succeeds, you know in the heart.
The early writers made poetry first take wings and soar;
Later writers have adorned their works
But each generation produces its own fine fruits
My principles were those of the Confucian school,
My mind has been on that path since my youth.
I regret I had no plan for my country . . .
I just sought a single branch to rest on . . .

Imaginary portrait of Du Fu by the artist Jiang Zhaohe (1904-1986). It was done in 1959 during Mao's Great Famine, one of China's most shattering disasters. The inscription says 'a thousand years have passed – who would have thought we are in a new age now, a myriad people singing together in happiness? Du Fu and I are experiencing such different emotions. How do I use my brush to portray his troubled brow?'

Select Bibliography

This is just a short note on the books about Du Fu, mainly in English, that I have particularly enjoyed and found helpful.

Florence Ayscough *Tu Fu: the Autobiography of a Chinese Poet*, I, 712-759 (Jonathan Cape, London 1929) and *Travels of a Chinese Poet* II AD 759-770 (Jonathan Cape, London 1934). Like Browning's Aeschylus, heroic, idiosyncratic, pioneering.

William Hung *Tu Fu: China's Greatest Poet* (Harvard UP, Cambridge Mass. 1952): still the best account of his life in English, or any European language. The supplementary volume (Harvard UP, Cambridge Mass. 1952) is invaluable for its notes.

David Hawkes *A Little Primer of Tu Fu* (Oxford University Press 1967); revised edition (Hong Kong 2016): delightful, an education in itself.

A. C. Graham *Poems of the Late T'ang* (Penguin Books 1965 and later editions); *New York Review of Books* 2008: magical.

A. R. Davis *Tu Fu* (Twayne, New York 1971) – an incisive and thoughtful account of the poet's life.

Eva Chou *Reconsidering Tu Fu* (Cambridge UP 1995): on the poet's later status as an icon.

Burton Watson *The Selected Poems of Du Fu* (Columbia University Press, New York 2002): a terrific introduction.

David Hinton *Awakened Cosmos* (Shambhala Publications Inc, Boulder 2019) and *The Selected Poems of Tu Fu* (New Directions, New York 2020): bold innovative, opening up new ways of seeing the poet.

Stephen Owen *The Great Age of Chinese Poetry: The High Tang* (Yale 1981, revised edition Melbourne and Basel 2013); *The Poetry of Du Fu* (de Gruyter 6 volumes Boston and Berlin 2016) – the first edition of all the poems in English.

The ongoing French edition by N. Chapuis: Du Fu *Oeuvres Poetique: I Poemes de Jeunesse* (Paris Belles Lettres 2015); II *La Guerre Civile* (755-759) 2018 III; *Au Bout du Monde* (759) 2021; Chapuis' edition totally bears out his idea that to help us read Chinese poetry, multiple translations are the way forward.

A short note on last phases (page 125): Theodor Adorno 'Late Style in Beethoven' (1937) in *Essays on Music* (Berkeley 2002); on Shakespeare Racine and Ibsen, *Last Periods* by Kenneth Muir (Liverpool 1961); on Michelangelo, Erich Heller *The Artist's Journey into the Interior and Other Essays* (Random House, New York 1965), and for a stimulating overview, Edward Said 'Thoughts on Late Style' in *London Review of Books* 5 August 2004.

On specific points: *The Three Perfections: Chinese Painting Poetry and Calligraphy* by Michael Sullivan (Thames & Hudson, London 1974) and Wu Hung 'Unearthing Wu Daozi (*c.*686 to *c.*760): The Concept of Authorship in Tang Painting' in *Art History* vol 45 issue 2 228-248 (April 2022).

On musical settings of Tang poetry: the website of John Thomson, www.silkqin.com.

The book does not perforce discuss how Chinese poetry works, metre, rhyme, etc. For an introduction, see David Hawkes's book and the discussion in A. C. Graham. On translation in general, Elliot Weinberger's fascinating *Nineteen Ways of Looking at Wang Wei* (New Directions, New York 1987), prints translations of a single poem, 'Deer Park' (new edition in 2016 with ten more ways).

On the ground, a special thanks to Nie Zuoping for his devoted tracking of the poet's journey from Tianshui to Chengdu (Southern Weekend 22 August 2019). And, finally, I must add my homage to the irrepressible traveller, translator and teacher, Bill Porter/Red Pine, whose *Finding Them Gone* (Port Townsend, Washington 2016) will delight all who wander the highways and byways of today's China seeking the traces of the ancient poets. Ganbei!

Index

Page references in *italics* indicate images.

Picture Credits

P2 Hu Zihan; PP6-7 ML Design; PP12-13 Visual China Group; P19 by author; P24 Cadbury Research Library: Special Collections, University of Birmingham; P25 ML Design; P27, P29, PP32-33, P34 Visual China Group; P37 Wikipedia; P39, P41, P43, P49 Visual China Group; P54 Pictures From History / Alamy Stock Photo; P67, P68 Visual China Group; PP70-71 MarsmanRom, Wikipedia; P73, P74 Visual China Group; P76 Pictures From History / Alamy Stock Photo; P78 Lu Yanshao; P80 Visual China Group; PP84-85, P87 Visual China Group; P88 Robert Heathman / Alamy Stock Photo; P91 LEJEANVRE Philippe / Alamy Stock Photo; P92 gazetteer still from author's collection; P98 ML Design; P101 photographs by G. Warren Swire. Images courtesy of John Swire & Sons Ltd and Special Collections, University of Bristol Library; P102 Visual China Group; P105, P109 from *The Yangtze Valley and Beyond* by Isabella Bird, John Murray, London 1899 (author's collection); P110 and cover John Thomson; PP106-7, 114-15, 120-121 126-127, 132-33, 142-3 from *The Grandeur of the Gorges* by Donald Mennie, Kelly and Walsh, Shanghai 1926, author's collection; P113 gazetteer still from author's collection; P129 Wikipedia Liaoning Provincial Museum, Shenyang; P130 The Picture Art Collection / Alamy Stock Photo; P134 ML Design; P136 Visual China Group; P139 Zhao Chuhui; PP144-145 Picture Library of Hunan; PP146-147 photograph by G. Warren Swire. Images courtesy of John Swire & Sons Ltd and Special Collections, University of Bristol Library; P150 by author; P153 Armand D' Angour; P157 Visual China Group; P160 Visual China Group; P162 Zeng Guohui; P163 Yang Xi; P169 by author; P170 Visual China Group; P172, P176, P191 by author/author's collection; P182 Pictures From History / Alamy Stock Photo.

Thanks

In addition, thanks to the publishers of the following titles for granting us permission to reproduce passages of text: Burton Watson, *The Selected Poems of Du Fu* (Columbia University Press, New York 2002); David Hinton, *Awakened Cosmos* (Shambhala Publications Inc. Boulder 2019); Stephen Owen *The Poetry of Du Fu* (de Gruyter, Boston and Berlin 2016).

Acknowledgements

In China, Professor Yang Yu of South Central University Changsha was very generous with her time and ideas. Cao Qin opened my eyes to the oral tradition in Changsha and sent me stories and recordings, and Deng Rongsheng shared his researches into the Du family in Hunan. Back in Britain at Simon and Schuster, my thanks to Ian Marshall who commissioned this book, and to Alison MacDonald, Victoria Godden and Laura Nickoll, and the designer Keith Williams; Martin Lubikowski drew the maps. My agent Catherine Clarke, Michele Topham, and all at FBA were, as always, a great support. At Maya Vision John Cranmer drafted maps and graphic ideas. Special thanks to Tina Li who for years now has been a great source of advice about Chinese texts and language, discussing many points of Du Fu's verse, along with handling the picture research. I must also thank Paul Hamilton for his kindness in reading my text and making many helpful suggestions; Armand D'Angour for his many insights and for providing a transcription of the musical setting for the Li Guinian poem, and Nicolas Chapuis for swapping ideas when in post in Beijing, and reading an early draft, and for his encouragement to a non-expert. Above all, fittingly in a labour of love, my thanks go to Rebecca Dobbs and Mina Wood who read the whole text through with great care and acuity and suggested countless improvements; without them the book would be much the poorer.

First published in Great Britain by Simon & Schuster UK Ltd, 2023

Editorial Director: Alison MacDonald
Project Editor: Laura Nickoll
Design: Keith Williams, sprout.uk.com

1 3 5 7 9 10 8 6 4 2

Simon & Schuster UK Ltd
1st Floor
222 Gray's Inn Road
London WC1X 8HB

www.simonandschuster.co.uk

Simon & Schuster Australia,
Sydney

www.simonandschuster.com.au

Simon & Schuster India,
New Delhi

www.simonandschuster.co.in

A CIP catalogue record for this book is available from the British Library

Hardback ISBN: 978-1-3985-1544-4
Ebook ISBN: 978-1-3985-1546-8

Printed and bound in Great Britain by Bell and Bain Ltd, Glasgow